COMMENTS FROM READERS

"I so enjoyed your ... piece in Business Marketing. I've also tried to deal with these issues .... Do keep up the good work."
> *George M. Naimark, Ph.D., President*
> *Naimark and Barba, Inc.*

"An engaging business memoir ... your technique of presenting the problems facing a small businessman in terms of concrete parables of your own experience is highly effective -- more effective, certainly to my mind, than generalized and stylized catch phrases and dry primers ..."
> *Scott Meredith, President*
> *Scott Meredith Literary Agency Inc.*

"Rarely ... do we have the pleasure of hearing from one who combines the CEO perspective on business with a healthy appreciation of using the communication process as a critical management tool."
> *Ray O'Connell, President*
> *Council of Communication Management*

"I read your Manager's Journal editorial ... with considerable interest. The circumstances rang familiar bells for me."
> *John P. Del Favero*
> *Delfco, Inc.*

"Your article in The Wall Street Journal ... was of particular interest to me because it mirrors so much my personal philosophy in the building of Marion Laboratories."
> *Ewing M. Kauffman, Chairman Emeritus*
> *Marion Merell Dow Inc.*

"Opening up my company is an option I have also considered, with the same type of reluctance you initially expressed in your article."
> *Steve Blake, President*
> *West Texas Printing Co., Inc.*

"We at the Dallas Group find ourselves in much the same situation and faced with similar problems you and your company were in (in) 1979. We found your article most enlightening ...."
> *David Dallas, Vice President*
> *The Dallas Group of America*

The author, a graduate of The University of Chicago, has been CEO of his own plastics materials business for 20 years. Under his stewardship the company experimented with a number of management methods. Since retirement, he has been contributing articles and essays on his business experience to business publications.

BUSINESS
NOT
AS USUAL

How to Win Managing a Company
Through Hard and Easy Times

By Hugh Aaron

STONES POINT PRESS
P.O. Box 384
Belfast, ME 04915

COVER by Imageset Design
EDITED by John A. Johnson

FIRST EDITION

Aaron, Hugh
Business Not As Usual: How to Win Managing a Company Through Hard and Easy Times
Library of Congress Catalog Card Number: 92-062348
ISBN 1-882521-00-5

$19.95 Softcover
Printed in the United States of America

We thank the editors and publishers for permission to reprint revised versions of the author's articles which originally appeared in their publications.

"Evening the Score of Caveat Emptor"
The Wall Street Journal (August 1990)
Copyright 1990 Dow Jones & Company, Inc.

"In Troubled Times, Run an Open Company"
as "Opening the Company"
The Wall Street Journal (December 1990)
Copyright 1990 Dow Jones & Company, Inc.

"Making the Most of a Recession"
Business Marketing (January 1991)
Copyright 1991 Crain Communications Inc.

"Recession Proofing a Company's Employees"
The Wall Street Journal (March 1991)
Copyright 1991 Dow Jones & Company, Inc.

"Be True to Yourself During Recession"
as "Coping with Recession: An Identity Crisis"
Plastics News (March 1991)
Copyright 1991 Crain Communications Inc.

"The Most Qualified Consultants I Would Ever Find"
as "The Managing Collective"
The Wall Street Journal (April 1991)
Copyright 1991 Dow Jones & Company, Inc.

"U.S. Business Relationships: Color Them Brutish"
as "Business: The Perpetual War"
The Wall Street Journal (June 1991)
Copyright 1991 Dow Jones & Company, Inc.

To

*my former employees
who put up with my idiosyncracies with a smile,
and who stuck by me through hard as well as easy times.*

Thanks to

*David Asman,
Editor of the Manager's Journal column of*
The Wall Street Journal,
*who first encouraged me to write
about my business experiences*

and to

*Dr. George M. Naimark,
for his moral support
during the composition of this book.*

... Hugh Aaron

Bumper Sticker:
I love my boss. I love my job.
I'm self-employed.

TABLE OF CONTENTS

CHAPTER I
THE FIRST YEARS

CHAPTER II
HUMAN RELATIONSHIPS

CHAPTER III
THE BUYOUT

CHAPTER IV
THE SUPREME TEST

CHAPTER V
MANAGING THROUGH RECESSION

CHAPTER VI
EXPERIMENTS IN MOTIVATION

CHAPTER VII
THE SALE

CHAPTER VIII
SOME VIEWS FROM A DISTANCE

EPILOGUE

APPENDIX

FOREWORD

It is common for authors of book introductions to say that they've known and admired the book's author for years. Not so here: until recently I didn't know Hugh Aaron from a Maine hole in the ground. I met him a year or so ago in the pages of *The Wall Street Journal;* the admiration dates from that introduction.

You see, I'm a business information junkie. I devour whatever I can, convinced as many of us are, that much of what we've been doing in business has been wrong-headed and needs to be jettisoned. In *Forbes, Harvard Business Review, Business Week, Fortune, Business Horizons,* books by the dozens by-you-know-who(m), and, of course, *The Wall Street Journal.* Enter Hugh Aaron.

I read one of Hugh's *Wall Street Journal* essays about his CEO experiences and was taken by its honesty, decency, logic and practicality. So into the permanent file, not recognizing the author's name, or even - I'm now embarrassed to admit - remembering it. About the fourth time this happened, I asked my secretary to get his address so that I could thank him for his unique contributions to the crowded business literature. Now you know.

Now, too, you have the opportunity to see why the prestigious *Wall Street Journal* has given so much space to Hugh Aaron's essays (9 as of this writing) and why so many strangers send him mash notes.

Here's just some of what you'll find in this book. First and foremost, the thoughtful observations and experiences of a CEO who faced, successfully, virtually all of the vicissitudes, challenges, frustrations and satisfactions of any business, of any size, in any business category. And with apologies to my friends in the academic world, here is the real blood, guts and giggles of running a business. This book, for example, strongly makes the point - regrettably underemphasized by some academics - that people really are the very essence of a business. *Really.*

More than that, Hugh Aaron used his company much as a scientist uses a laboratory: to test his hypotheses against reality and, by so doing, was willing to challenge his intuitive sense, was willing to discover that his instincts might be wrong. Many such experiments were conducted and much knowledge was gained.

The beauty part of all this: so much of what he learned is generalizable; his life, our gain. Your move.

GEORGE M. NAIMARK, Ph.D.

Dr. Naimark, a management consultant, has been a director of seven companies and is president of Naimark & Barba, Inc., *Florham Park, NJ. He has written for management, marketing, advertising, scientific and medical journals and has authored two books:* COMMUNICATIONS on COMMUNICATIONS *and* A PATENT MANUAL FOR SCIENTISTS AND ENGINEERS.

PREFACE

For 16 years after graduating college I was somebody's employee. During that time I held more than 20 jobs, among them, waiter in a restaurant, quality control technician, office manager, printing facility supervisor, plastic materials salesman and manager of a small manufacturing division of a large corporation. I rarely lasted more than two or three years on a job - more often less than a year, usually because I would be critical of the way the company was managed.

I saw that most managements either denied the truth about what was happening or they chose to ignore it. When I suggested change the boss consistently shot down my ideas. Eventually I would be fired or I'd quit to search for that "holy grail," the enlightened, progressive company.

But in those 16 years of tumult I learned, if slowly, how not to manage a company, and that I had to be my own master. I learned to face the truth no matter how unpleasant or devastating it might be. This often meant accepting responsibility for bad decisions, not only mine but other's as well. When a recession struck, it would have been easy to sit back and say, "I'm not responsible. Nothing can be done." I could easily have blamed my workers for their poor productivity. But blaming others, blaming fate, blaming forces beyond my control, would have been irresponsible.

With hardly a penny to my name I joined three cohorts in a business venture that for the next nine years endured one crisis after another. I found contending with partners draining and inhibiting, but in the tenth year, after buying out the last partner, with my employees as stockholders, I was then free to experiment with a long list of innovative management ideas. The company thus became a virtual management laboratory until it was sold ten years later.

The chapters that follow comprise an autobiographical account of my failures and successes in roughly chronological order from the first days to the last in dealing with both the company's problems and my own privately as CEO. As best I could, I have tried to be objective and honest. My theme throughout the book is: accept responsibility for what happens; face the truth no matter how brutal it is; and don't expect to find quick fixes and easy solutions.

If the reader should find these experiences and my message helpful in his or her own pursuit of solutions to business problems, I would be gratified.

HUGH AARON

CHAPTER I

THE FIRST YEARS

Why I Went Into Business - The True Story

The small publicly held company on Long Island was in trouble, running out of cash - and worse yet, bank credit. Only the tiny satellite division I managed in New England made a profit, and that was being drained off. In effect we were the child supporting the parent. Barely two years old, the division was producing a then-innovative product. It allowed the fabricator of a plastic item such as a toy to color plastic material at one third the cost of the usual method.

Meanwhile, a large, rich, publicly held company in New York had opened a facility in Atlanta to produce the same type of product. Management at that facility, after encountering two years of mounting losses, had become desperate. The necks of the brass were in jeopardy.

It was then they approached me to identify and solve their problems. I was offered a hefty salary and a vague executive position. Having lost confidence in the company for which I worked, I was interested. However, I rejected the offer, suggesting instead I work as a consultant for an hourly fee. My thought was to raise enough capital and start my own business. But after the company upped the salary offer and defined my future more favorably, I took the job.

The plant was in an industrial suburb but its administrative staff worked from the luxurious offices of a downtown sky-scraper. I resided, at company expense, in a high-rise hotel nearby. On my first tour of the plant, I was overwhelmed by its enormous scale and impressed by its array of equipment of which the manager was justifiably proud. I was bewildered at the sight of its sophisticated lab which included a costly state-of-the-art analog computer. The operation was obviously the realization of an engineer's dream. By comparison my old operation was back in the dark ages - but it made money.

By the time the tour was over I knew certain things were wrong:

*The company had designed the plant for lengthy production runs, but the market was still young and orders for large volumes were rare.

*At the same time, due to the size and sophistication of the equipment, the cleandown and setup time between runs was so excessive that machines were more often down than producing.

*The company was bent on pursuing a single market almost exclusively: the highly competitive and fickle automotive field which imposed strict specifications on its suppliers and showed no mercy when breached.

After a few weeks I also observed:

*More time and labor were required to formulate products by means of the computer than the old fashioned way. Moreover, the formulations were often inferior. Computer formulating, then in its infancy, obviously had a way to go.

*The plant consistently failed to meet delivery dates, ignoring the precept that the service aspect of the business is just as important as its product. Customers needed color when they said they needed it or they would shut down.

*It was obvious the plant manager, the engineers and the upper echelon sales and administrative vice-presidents were blindly committed to running a technologically ultimate plant, not the lean and flexible type of operation needed to serve the existing markets. They wanted a showplace to which they could invite their automotive prospects.

A month passed. I familiarized myself with all details of the operation, its many levels of personnel (the actual pecking order) and the politics of the organization. However, I delayed drafting the awaited analysis and proposal until I learned who had been responsible for what feature of the past. I needed to know who, having a stake in the status quo, would become my nemesis. But the brass in New York urged me on, promising to "let the chips fall where they may." Thus, I was fooled and discovered the enemy too late.

Holed up in my hotel room for an entire week, I wrote more than 100 well considered hand-written pages describing what was wrong and what remedial steps should be taken. I turned it in to be typed. I heard nothing. Finally, three weeks later the brass in New York ordered me to hightail it up there.

Upon entering the division vice president's office I saw my manuscript, still in its hand-written form, lying on his otherwise barren desk. What was I trying to do? he demanded, waving the sheets of paper in my face. He didn't stop there. I was "ridiculous." Didn't I realize I was virtually condemning the entire operation and prescribing they start over? Retract it. Give him something sensible, less radical. Be reasonable.

I insisted I did what I was hired to do: write the truth as I saw it. Anything else, even taming it down, would be dishonest. His secretary entered with a glass of milk which he drank right down. Look, he said, even if I were right, everyone - the manager, the engineers, the marketing and sales people, himself, his boss - would be at risk were my paper to see the light of day.

My initial contempt turned to pity and I proposed he bury the paper and forget it was ever written. But I told him if they didn't do as I suggested he and his associates would still be in trouble. We shook hands and he placed his arm over my shoulder in a genuinely friendly gesture. That Friday my check included severance pay. Twice burned, I knew then I had to become my own master.

[As postscript, in less than a year, the division vice-president and all his cohorts were fired and, indeed, eventually so was the president.]

Getting Started

That first day in my own business, I felt like a man unbound. Until then I didn't know how frustrating my life as an employee had been. On that day my feet were marvelously light. I seemed taller than before. I breathed pure oxygen. No one could tell me what I must do. The future was as open as the sky and I was a soaring rocket.

But it was never the same again. Reality quickly closed in. I soon discovered I had entered a race against unmerciful time.

For years as an employee lacking capital I waited for an opportunity to present itself. I had devised a plan to start an operation making coloring products for the plastics industry. I resolved I wouldn't do so until I possessed all the prerequisites for success.

As it happened, it all came together seemingly overnight.

*I had the manufacturing know-how. After managing a similar operation for a division of a large corporation I knew the business in detail, how to formulate and manufacture the product, what equipment to buy.

*I had a superior product with distinct advantages. New to the market, color concentrates provided the customer a less costly method of coloring plastic than the standard one in use. It also offered the customer an opportunity to reduce his raw material inventory.

*I had knowledge of the market. Having for several years been a salesman for the division, I knew the territory intimately.

*I had a supply of talent - three willing partners. A distinct advantage I thought. One was skilled at production, one was rich but silent, one was a super-salesman and I was a pretty good administrator.

*I had the necessary capital. Not only did the rich partner furnish the startup money, his father-in-law was on the board at the bank, a valuable connection.

*The timing was good. In 1966 the plastics industry was relatively young and booming at a faster clip than the already upbeat economy.

However, as the months passed, one by one these prerequisites proved to be less genuine than I anticipated.

As for manufacturing know how, our equipment proved to be insufficient to make a product that would meet the quality standards of fussier customers. Thus, we were limited to a low-priced, narrow segment of the market.

As for superior product, ours worked poorly in customers' automated handling devices due to an irregular granulated form dictated by our process.

As for the supply of talent, the production partner chose to work banker's hours and began an affair with his female assistant; the super-salesman partner, a lover of boats, devoted most of his time to managing a marina in which he had invested.

As for the necessary capital, the rich partner was rich only by virtue of having married a rich woman who clung to her wealth. Thus, as our losses mounted and it became evident we needed more equipment to tailor our products to the demands of the market, the rich partner refused to put up additional capital.

As for knowledge of the market, most customers, even those we had counted on, were reluctant to buy from a new business with unproven staying power. The catch: we were denied the very orders our business needed in order to remain the reliable source the trade required. The only thing right about our venture was the timing, but that seemed of little benefit. I saw doom on the horizon.

At the end of the first year, the company showed a negative net worth and a loss equivalent to 50 percent of gross sales. Meanwhile, I had been working 12 hours a day, six days a week for almost nothing. When a large firm offered me a substantial salary to set them up in the business and run it, I told the rich partner (who owned controlling interest) I would quit. He pleaded that I remain two months to the end of the quarter, as if in that time he expected a miracle. He would not accept bankruptcy, he said, due to his pride.

I escaped to the shore, walked the beach and formulated a proposal which I presented to him. If I bought out the two useless partners for a nominal sum, would he give me a sufficient number of his shares to make me a 50 percent owner? Should they refuse my terms, I would leave. He promptly agreed. The others protested, but I remained adamant and had my way.

Before the quarter ended the company experienced its first month's profit. A miracle? Not really. In fact it was the first fruits of my year-long effort of faithfully calling on the trade. It seems a year was enough to convince customers we were going to last.

The other company's offer was still there and enticing. But I had concluded during my walk on the beach that above all I wanted my own business. Given the freedom to be my own master, the incentive to receive reward for my risk and my labor, and to be rid of the handicap of unproductive partners, I would stick it out to a happy or unhappy end.

For the next 20 years, until it was sold, the company never experienced a red bottom line again. Though my rich partner wouldn't put up more money, his signature was golden (unlike mine in the beginning) at the bank where we secured loans to purchase better equipment to make the products I knew we could sell. What it took to succeed had come together.

Years later when my partner and I had a falling out, my decision returned to haunt me. Though I was in the driver's seat back then, I was timid. With no record of success I lacked self-confidence. I had made the error of not demanding control.

Reflections on Being an Entrepreneur

A few months after being in business I discovered an entrepreneur's life is radically different from that of ordinary mortals. As an entrepreneur, every act, every decision I made, was rational, even when rational solutions weren't called for - as, for example, when dealing with people. For another thing, I was keenly aware the consequences of every decision would eventually be revealed in a single composite figure with stunning clarity: the bottom line. And third, I was fanatical in trying to direct the course of events towards specific business goals - an activity that was often fruitless.

These entrepreneurial characteristics - the CEO's rationality, the profit figure as the measure of performance, and the relentless dedication to a single purpose - had profound effects on my physical and mental states and my relationship with my family. These ranged from stomach problems to anxiety attacks to divorce. Clearly, the entrepreneur's life is an intense form of existence.

As a novice businessman, I became convinced that mindless, entropic forces prevailed whose sole purpose was to undermine my attempts to keep the business in the black. Too many prospective customers refused to cooperate and do business with us. Those who did refused to accept our prices lying down. The competitors refused to know their place and steer clear of my customers. The vendors refused to budge on price and insisted on impossible 30-day terms. Then there were employees who didn't show up to service that emergency order or who quit just at the long-awaited moment of achieving peak job performance.

Obviously it was a conspiracy devised by the cruel, hostile world of free enterprise. The business was like a child that, left to its own devices, would damage itself. To survive, it had to be nurtured and guided by a doting parent: me. Until I took this point of view, that of the parent to the child, I was in constant turmoil, outraged by the people and events that sought to weaken my company's health. But like any neurotic parent, I too did things - with the best intentions, of course - that had a deleterious effect on the enterprise. As with any parent-child relationship, the business mirrors the CEO's personality: a neurotic parent is bound to spawn a neurotic child.

One example of my inept parenting is typical. When the business was in its infancy I was over-protective. Why not? Wasn't it totally dependent on me? When it became an adolescent and acquired a number of employees, it began asserting itself and taking off in directions that weren't always in its own best interest. For example, our receivables might be allowed to languish too long and cause a cash flow problem, or our equipment would continually break due to insufficient maintenance. Yet I refused to let go, to acknowledge others could bring the operation under control. I was slow to delegate and let the employees do the day-to-day directing.

My pride was another example of parental incompetence. As the child achieved a measure of success, I ignored caution and egged it on to expand as if there were no limits, as if the thriving economy would endure forever and held no danger. Then a virus struck: a deep recession. After an operation, and the removal of some parts, without which death would have been certain, it slowly regained its health and I found humility.

Though the child grew into a confident adult, I reserved one aspect of control for myself: keeping it on track. Even in our personal lives, staying on track is a life-long problem. (Genius is the result of doing so better than anyone else.) In my pre-entrepreneurial days I was easily distracted from whatever path I was on. But without a bottom line to reckon with, staying on track was never a matter of life or death as it is with a business. Every instance in which the business digressed, such as pursuing markets in which our expertise was limited or entering into unrelated fields, such as equipment that would enable our customers to dispense our plastic coloring products, the results never justified the time, energy and money invested.

Staying on track involved more than keeping an enterprise headed in a consistent direction. As in raising a child, a business must follow certain rules and procedures. Since people tend to break rules and abjure procedures, I soon became a law and order fanatic. But under this yoke, initiative and daring declined and we seemed to stagnate. Against my nature, I loosened up and allowed a little chaos in. Clearly staying on track was a balancing act. I told myself it was OK, even beneficial, to veer a little off center to make things exciting and keep everyone alert.

The child/adult metaphor breaks down at a certain point in the life cycle of a business. An enterprise may grow old, even inefficient and senile, but the right doctor can restore it. I guided my business through infancy to comfortable old age in which it could take life easy as it reaped the benefits of its 20-year struggle. But I knew it couldn't rest for long. I knew that, unlike myself in whom the aging process was irreversible, the business had the capacity to recapture the innovative surge of its middle years. So I sold my aged child and gave it an opportunity for renewal. Lo and behold, a few years later, I learned the business had given birth to a few satellites. Now in my mid-60s I'm a proud grandfather. Frankly, I wouldn't want it any other way.

What Makes an Entrepreneur Go

Entrepreneurs are fanatics. Their drive, above all, makes the enterprise succeed. Even after failure, the best of them refuse to submit. They try again and again. Throughout most of my entrepreneurship I was well aware of my extreme determination to make it and to keep the enterprise on a secure path. So were the people that had to deal with me. I never understood where the drive came from. Was I born driven or was it the result of my upbringing?

Now, having left the struggle behind, I can speculate on the source. Though my story is unique, as is everyone's, it may also contain a universal thread.

I distinguish between entrepreneur and corporate executive. The former engages in risk and thrives on change. The latter fears risk and prefers the status quo. Both seek security, but by different means. The staid corporate executive's role is suffocating to the entrepreneur; the entrepreneur's role is threatening to the corporate executive. Occasionally both roles are melded within the same person, but not often enough. A business often outgrows the entrepreneur's capacity to lead. The established corporation often loses the innovative spark the entrepreneur brings to a business.

I can attribute my familiarity with owning a business to my father, a dedicated small businessman. From childhood I felt being in business was my destiny. I thought I might run my father's upholstering shop. Yet early on I chose to work for someone else - the safe strategy.

Looking back, it wasn't such a bad idea. From those experiences, I learned the right and the wrong way to manage a business. Eventually joining my father, I found we didn't work well together and I again went to work for someone else. For many more years the idea of being on my own nagged at me, though I hadn't the faintest idea of how I'd do it. I wasn't particular. Any kind of business would do so long as I could make it grow. By the time I took the leap, I was already 42. But facts don't explain my need, my compulsion to be independent.

Owning a business satisfied my specific preferences in dealing with life. I wished to be in control, to "call the shots." It troubled me to be subjected to the vicissitudes of circumstances and events. I needed to have input. I required perfection from myself and near perfection from those around me. There was no room for error in my world. It was hard on those dealing with me.

Underlying this was a basic distrust of the world. I didn't suspect conspiracy or feel paranoid, but I believed I couldn't always rely on people. Events were often adverse. Indeed, when conditions were salutary for a while, they became suspect and I awaited the sword to fall. I was alert to an ever-present threat: chaos. But, above all, I wanted to trust. The conflict between my view of reality and my wish to have it otherwise was a constant source of frustration and error.

Such was the way I was - and still am. However, now the environment is more peaceful and less stressful. The question is: why. To understand often means to forgive. The entrepreneur can't avoid causing others pain. It's the nature of business. To seek control, to distrust the world, to strive for perfection are the hallmarks of most entrepreneurs and leaders. My case may be special only to a point.

At four, I experienced the trauma of a lengthy separation from doting parents. I felt abandoned. When I finally returned home I found myself "replaced" by a newborn brother. To a four-year-old this was betrayal of the first order.

I would never trust my parents again, yet I wanted nothing more. I can remember resolving to find a way to escape my enforced dependency, insisting I didn't need others in order to survive. It took me 38 years to achieve that goal.

But I did need others. I couldn't succeed by myself so I created a new family - my company - that I fathered and made prosper and protected against the cruel warriors of fate and competition. The business was my private kingdom. It provided me the emotional security I had been seeking most of my life.

Every entrepreneur, I suspect, has a similar story to tell that would reveal the birth of his or her drive to be independent, in control and leading an organization of human beings down a safe path. Of course, the entrepreneur is far more complicated than I have depicted. Creativity, the love of challenge, solving problems and an eternal optimism are inherent in the entrepreneurial personality. These are substantially genetic gifts. Combine them with the right measure of neurosis: voila, we have an entrepreneur par excellence. Unfortunately - or perhaps, fortunately - not many of us qualify.

The CEO'S Reward

Any man or woman who leaves a secure, well-paying job to start a small business has just made the least business-like decision in his or her entrepreneurial career. It borders on the irrationality of choosing a marriage partner. Even then we generally know what to expect from a spouse. But what do we expect from a business?

Is it money? God forbid. During my early years in business making money for myself was the last thing on my mind. In fact, at one point I was convinced I'd never do as well as I would have had I remained an employee on the rise with my previous corporate employer. Although after 10 years in business my salary far exceeded any sum I had imagined possible, it was never a goal, never a motivator. Had my salary been cut 75 percent, it wouldn't have mattered. In fact, during lean times I routinely reduced my personal income while increasing that of our employees. Small business CEO's often do that.

When I read of the increases in already enormous salaries and benefits paid CEO's of large corporations, especially those with a history of negative performance, I feel outraged. It demeans the principle of reward for excellence. It also devalues a far deeper precept underlying the relationship between the CEO and his or her company: that of personal commitment. (Hired CEOs of large corporations should be paid only moderate salaries in combination with their company's stock held in escrow until departure or retirement.)

As in marriage, the prized feature a business offers the CEO is the opportunity of commitment. It provides a purpose, an entity on which to focus one's heart, mind and soul. It is the object of the CEO's loyalty and dedication. With this the CEO discovers a freedom known nowhere else. Money is incidental - simply a measure of success. It is not the reward a committed CEO seeks - or needs.

In its practical application, the relationship of a fully committed CEO to his or her company is similar to that of the CEO to his or her spouse and family. The CEO comes after the company, after the employees, after the creditors, after the customers, after the stockholders. To reverse the relationship - to have the CEO come first - is destructive to the company.

While the CEO can rationalize he or she deserves an extravagant salary or frequent afternoons on the golf course or on the yacht are good for business, associates see it as selfishness and even betrayal. The employees, sensing the way it is, can't be blamed for withholding their devotion to the company's cause. The creditors, feeling used, may well become skeptical and demanding. The customers sooner or later grasp the one-sidedness of what should be a mutually beneficial transaction and go elsewhere. And the stockholders are bound to stop trusting and become irate. Such unhappy reactions may not occur all at once, but in time they're inevitable. The CEO's violations of duty destroy the underpinnings of the business like hidden dry rot. Indeed, such a person has no business being in business.

As costly as unjustifiable rewards to a CEO can be to a large corporation, it can be even more devastating to a partnership. If one business partner is motivated by money and the other by a sublime dedication to the business, they will find themselves at odds. A crisis usually develops which inevitably tests the relationship. During a period of increasing losses, when I suggested my equal partner and I cut our salaries in half, he refused. Yet my need to help the company was such I unilaterally reduced my salary anyway.

My partner and I differed radically on how we viewed the company, vis-a-vis ourselves. From his point of view, the company existed solely for the owners - us. I had a much larger vision of the company. For me the company existed not only for the owners but also for the employees, the customers, the suppliers, the community, the nation and the world. To my partner I was absurd, a dreamer. To me he was self-centered and short sighted.

In retrospect, I see our business approach reflected our views of life. He felt the world was there to be used for his benefit. I felt the world belonged to the future as well as the present, and I was merely renting it while I lived. He was a consumer, I was a conserver.

Ironically, the difference in business approach between us, both American born and raised, replicates the difference between many older cultures and ours. Japanese CEOs, for instance, earn far less than their American counterparts. Their managements take the long view of their companies' future. Their dedication to the advancement of their companies' welfare is well known. In general, there's less hype and more substance, less arrogance and more flexibility in their business approach than in ours. The long-run success of the enterprise is intrinsic to the reward their top business people seek.

To this long-range oriented, dedicated visionary, the reward is in the doing, in getting there, in surmounting the challenges. As for the money, I like it as much as anybody else, but by itself it's a mediocre and unsatisfying motivator.

Business Success: Luck or Ability

"You've been lucky." This is the sentiment some people have expressed concerning my 20-year career as CEO. I can't disagree. Though the company came close to failing twice, a bitter partnership battle transpired, and our biggest customer, whose business comprised one third of our sales, deserted us, we survived and eventually prospered. Certainly luck helped.

When I originally assumed ownership of our factory building, I had no idea it would become a collateral vehicle for buying out a recalcitrant partner. Nor did I realize when I hired a particular manager he had the creative ability to invent a new, patentable product that would help stanch declining sales. And I could never have dreamed the company I worked for 30 years before (and from whom I had been dismissed) would covet our product line and expertise and acquire us. Luck, good fortune, fortuitous events for which I can take no credit undeniably played a major role in all this. But what about the bad luck, the disasters, the multiple machine breakdowns, the fires, the costly failure of our process cooling system, the 21 percent interest rate, the surprise departure of three key employees who, armed with our secret formulas and prices, set up their own business in competition with us? At one point things got so bad that when good things happened we assumed they were aberrations. What about the false rumors our company was near bankruptcy, the impossible payoffs demanded by certain corporate purchasing agents, the ethnic prejudice directed against us by certain prospective customers, the destruction wrought by the dishonesty of certain of our own managers? I find it equally difficult to attribute the cause of these bad events to myself.

In spite of ill fortune, we succeeded. It would seem luck played only a partial role in determining our destiny. After all, luck cuts both ways. Of course there's the person who wins a fortune in the lottery, but for most of us, luck, good and bad, usually occurs in small bits and pieces.

If luck weren't the only player during my 20 years as CEO, from the inception of the company to its sale, did I, at various crossroads, make more right decisions than wrong ones? In retrospect I can identify which key decisions proved to be good and which bad, though at the time I couldn't be sure how they would turn out. Still, I was there and I deliberately made things happen - more often for better than worse, even if accidentally.

Luck aside, credit must be given to the CEO who is on the scene making decisions. The question is, what makes them the right ones?

*Operating under the handicap of uncertainty, yes entropy, the successful CEO possesses courage - the courage to be wrong. This is what is implied in the old saw: better a wrong decision than none at all. At least a wrong decision is certain, while "no decision" leaves matters to chaos, the blight of rationality. And business aspires above all else to be rational in order to minimize risk.

*The successful CEO has the acumen to recognize an opportunity and to take advantage of it. It's likely even the most competent CEOs miss more opportunities than they will ever know, but it only takes a few opportunities, often only one, on which to build success.

*To a successful CEO every problem is solvable (whether it really is or not), a tasty challenge to his or her creative imagination. In business school the student learns the rational approach to managing and the tools at his or her disposal. This information and these techniques are, of course, highly useful. But they neither substitute nor compensate for the creative imagination which one either has or doesn't have and which can't be learned. Back in the late 1940s no school taught Taiichi Ohno of Toyota the concept of lean production; it came from within him. Indeed it is the freedom to apply one's creative imagination to problems or advantages generated by luck that can be the most rewarding aspect of being at the top.

*Some CEOs have the uncanny ability to forecast the future better than others. From knowledge of human behavior and an analysis of past and current events, such persons can intuitively predict what is likely to happen under various circumstances. It is this capacity, which the CEO usually knows he has, and which others soon come to acknowledge, that gives him the edge in making correct decisions. Many failed businessmen, having no such capacity, no clue to the possible consequences of their actions, habitually plunge blindly into a miasma of uncertainty.

*While the successful CEO may have certain special abilities that are crucial to success, he or she probably lacks others just as crucial. A CEO's recognition of his or her limitations is fundamental, but this alone isn't enough. The effective CEO surrounds himself or herself with people possessing the strengths he or she lacks. I hired strong sales people because I was weak in that role. Also, being a somewhat compulsively ordered administrator, I chose executives who were more laid back than I.

*As important as the above imperatives are to business success, they pale beside that of a CEO's single mindedness of purpose. The successful CEO, at least during a phase of his or her reign, is a virtual fanatic, dedicated to the company's survival - often at high personal cost. The successful CEO knows no limitations regarding hours, responsibilities and functions that might lead to a desired goal. Such a CEO is driven, needing autonomy, and under compulsion to control subordinates and events. Though the CEO may be hard on others, even impossible to some, such a person is still an effective leader.

Of course not all CEO's have these characteristics in equal measure. In many instances employees compensate for their absence. No matter, it is their presence, regardless in whom they reside, that counts.

Can an aspiring businessperson not possessing the six features I have described, depend on luck to effect his or her success? I submit that person would be doomed to failure. Upon reviewing my 20-year experience as CEO, and weighting the role luck played versus executive ability in our company's modest success, I would give the former a 10 and the latter a 90.

One might say these values apply only in my case. But, based on my 16 years as an employee with many companies, I believe our company's struggle, regardless of the specifics, is typical. In most businesses the failures and triumphs attributable to luck and ability generally occur in the same proportion as ours. To state the obvious: companies with good managers usually succeed; companies with bad managers rarely do.

Government: Friend or Adversary

It was 1957. I was sitting across the desk from the district commissioner in the lower Manhattan office of the Federal Trade Commission pleading for the survival of my infant gold-plating company. It was my first business venture.

For months I had been calling on jewelry, watch case, and trophy firms all across Manhattan trying to sell our new gold-plating service. It involved a newly patented process that enabled us to electrolytically apply a gold plate to any desired thickness upon a base metal. My partner, the technical expert, was granted the sole rights to use the process throughout the Western Hemisphere.

Prospective customers were interested but cautious. Hoping to break into an established market, we offered prices that seemed too good to be true.

Until then, in the United States, gold could be electrolytically applied to a base metal in a thickness of only one micron or less. It was called a flash plate. Greater thicknesses had to be applied mechanically, a more expensive technique known as "gold filled" or "rolled gold plate." Flash-plating was common in junk jewelry and had poor wearing qualities. The mechanical method was used in more expensive items.

In a month we began receiving small orders. I'd pick up the customer's base metal goods at his or her shop and return them in a day or two beautifully plated with the micron thickness and process name impressed into an unobtrusive location on the surface of the plated object. Word spread, the number of orders increased and we were looking forward to a shining future. Then one day we received a fateful call from a customer: Did we realize it was unlawful to designate our process other than a flash plate?

If we couldn't identify the process for what it was, specify the gold thickness especially, then it would obviously be mistaken for flash-plate. The customer couldn't be sure of our gold thickness claims, nor could he sell his plated object on such a basis. I rushed to the Federal Trade Commission in panic.

The local commissioner indicated any electrolytically applied coating fell into the category of a flash-plate. After I pointed out watches were being imported from Switzerland with marks similar to ours (made by the very Swiss firm that had licensed us), he suggested we file a complaint. But we wished only to compete with the imported products. He warned the FTC would issue a cease and desist order were we to continue and urged us to pressure our representatives in Washington to change the law.

The next day I visited a specialist in regulatory law, a lawyer on Park Avenue. No doubt the rules inhibit competition, he said, which is not the government's intent. We had justifiable grounds for seeking a change. However we'd be bucking the Gold Filled Association. The group had a powerful lobby in Washington and the cost of fighting it could run well into six figures, a sum far beyond our meager means.

Thus my partner and I were forced to close our venture. I returned to New England where my wife had remained while I was trying to get the business established. My partner took off for Santiago, Chile, where he became wealthy, in part by using the process. It was my first experience with government regulation. From then on I remained wary of government.

I've experienced only one salutary relationship with a government agency, the Small Business Administration (SBA). Even this was somewhat shady at the beginning. Only after hiring an intervenor, an influential lawyer friend of my partner's, were we able to secure our first loan.

In subsequent years our company had difficulties twice with the IRS. The first incident occurred during an audit in which the agent disallowed motel expenses incurred while staying overnight in a resort area. After I proved, with considerable difficulty, I had called on a major customer who was vacationing nearby did he change his mind. I had learned, however, when dealing with a government agency, contrary to civil law, innocence has to be proven rather than guilt.

The second incident concerned a deduction for our anti-pollution devices. Despite our persistent protest, the IRS refused to allow it, though admitting the law was gray. Rather than undergo the expense of seeing the issue through the tax court, we paid.

We also had a problem with a state sales tax audit. The agent claimed we owed a tax on the interior air pollution equipment installed to conform to OSHA requirements. Armed with a copy of the law exempting such equipment, we appealed and won.

Prior to its installation, OSHA had fined us for not having the equipment, though it had been ordered and was in the process of being designed and built months before the agency had appeared at our door. On appealing to the district director, we pointed out that having proved our intention to be in compliance, we were being punished unfairly. Would he as a father also punish a child who shows contrition and promises to mend his ways? During our meeting we received no satisfaction. But later the fine was forgiven.

Except for local government with whom we could usually reason, our company found government regulators threatening and adversarial. We were lawful and substantial taxpayers, happy to contribute our share to the community, the state and the nation. But from our vantage point it seemed the government was willing to "kill the goose that laid the golden egg." Why, we often wondered, couldn't the government view us as we viewed our customers - a source of sustenance, in which their and our interests were mutual?

The Free Enterprise System - At What Price?

When I worked for someone else and my boss would say, "I love the Free Enterprise system, but I'd love it more if I had a monopoly," I always laughed. Not until I had my own business did I fully appreciate what he meant. Now that the Communist system has been discredited, it follows that the Free Enterprise system is being touted as the world's nirvana. But, as CEO of my own company I soon learned it's far from it. For all the freedom it allows, for all the opportunity it affords, it demands a price, sometimes one so high as to be life threatening. We, the Free Enterprise businessmen of the world should, in all fairness, level with the closed societies who have chosen to adopt our system. We should tell them what they're in for.

When I began in business, there were few competitors serving the market. Within a year after we established our staying power, we grew exponentially. Those were heady days: our prices were rarely questioned. Within five years all that changed and we were fighting - by lowering prices and improving service - to retain the business we had.

It was very hard on the nerves.

I knew life would never be the same again as a long period of employee turnover began. By letting our weaker performing workers and staff members go, we sought through painful trial and error to develop a corps of superior ones. Tension and insecurity abounded. The perpetrators of mistakes were castigated because our costs no longer allowed for error. The system demanded we forsake a portion of our humanity. Rationality ruled. We mercilessly beat down our suppliers to their rock bottom prices, and we delayed paying our vendors for as long as we could. If we didn't call it war, we took the attitude that every employee, every customer, every vendor, every government, (local, state and federal) was our enemy. After all, each entity either tried to charge us more than we wished to pay, or pay us less than we wished to charge. That's the way the Free Enterprise system works.

It's very hard on the nerves.

Then we had several close calls towards disaster - a recession now and then for instance. The Free Enterprise economy is a sneaky thing: it lulls you into complacency then strikes at your heart without warning like a coiled snake.

It's very hard on the nerves.

Then we had a partnership war which was no less trying and destructive than a bitter divorce. With private ownership such possibilities are rife. It took years to recover from the damage.

It's very hard on the nerves.

Then several key employees banded together and defected to form their own business in competition with us. Such spawning of companies is endemic to the Free Enterprise system. I couldn't even be angry. Hadn't I left my former employer to do the same thing?

But it was hard on the nerves.

Then a major account left us to produce our products in-house after we had expanded our capacity to better serve it; over 30 percent of our sales was lost in one stroke. Nowhere is it written in the Free Enterprise system that a customer should be considerate of or forthright with its suppliers.

Yes, it's very hard on the nerves.

Then you arrive home after a long, tense day at the shop and your wife complains you devote too little time to the family; business comes first. You argue the business is in trouble and needs your attention. It's always in trouble, she says. The business places the food on the table, you counter, and pays the rent. You reach an impasse.

It never stops being hard on the nerves.

Despite it all, we were able enough warriors to defeat the opposing forces, or at least to hold them off. Finally, after 15 years of riding a wave of frenzied peaks and dull valleys, we struck a decent period of persistent stability - the Reagan era. Indeed, for the first time in our history our company began accumulating more cash than we needed.

Not being used to this, it was somewhat hard on the nerves. Should we save the cash to tide us over the next recession or should we use it to grow? No question a recession was bound to occur sooner or later. But if we didn't invest in ourselves we were bound to slide backwards. The competition certainly wasn't letting up. That's how it is with the Free Enterprise system.

Then, as my income rose to over 16 times that of our workers, I had a sense first-hand of the grossly unequal distribution of wealth the Free Enterprise system promotes. True, I had taken the risk and suffered through the most terrifying downs, but I knew I didn't do it for the money. I did it because I needed to prove I could. I wanted to be independent and able to react. That freedom is the most valuable contribution to the individual and society the Free Enterprise system offers.

As the company's wealth increased, I shared it through an all-employee stock ownership plan, generous benefits and incentives for extra performance. None of the employees seemed to mind my affluence. Rather they accepted it as well earned. Most knew they wouldn't take the risk I did. And some, especially those who were still young and wished to control part of their destiny, might yet try their hand at it. To them the Free Enterprise System is highly inviting. I must warn them, be prepared: it'll be mighty hard on the nerves.

CHAPTER II

HUMAN RELATIONSHIPS

The Myth of Indispensability

When our company was young and very small, we weren't technologically superior. Our process was fairly common and our products routine. But our quick response to customers' demands gave us an edge against the competition. Our superiority resided in the performance of a few employees, especially in their skillful formulation and manufacturing of flawless custom products - colors for plastics.

Our lab technician, a born color formulator, was especially outstanding. All of us, the workers, the office staff, myself as CEO, and the salesmen, were awed by this young man's uncanny ability. We considered him our resident genius. I often worried about our fate were he to become ill. Everyone considered him indispensable.

Before we could produce a product, the lab first had to develop a recipe, compose a sample quantity and submit it to the customer for trial and approval. Thus our capacity to service a customer's order depended on the accuracy and speed at which the sample could be prepared. Most competitors' labs were so backed up customers often had to wait weeks for samples to arrive before they could evaluate them and place orders. It was a universal industry bottleneck. In our case, we could satisfy most requests in a week or less.

For the first two years our technician was able to keep up simply by working more hours. As the company grew and more demands were placed on the lab, we urged him to hire qualified assistants. We didn't mean "hands." Those were already in place performing routine work. We wanted technicians of his own caliber or near it. He balked, insisting he could easily cope with the mounting demand.

Soon he was working 12 hours a day including Saturdays and sometimes Sundays. Eventually, feeling harried, he grew irritable and uncooperative. This led to management's fear he would become exhausted and rendered ineffective. Furthermore, realizing the success of the enterprise was so dependent on the skill of one man concerned us. Though still recognized as a genius, his colleagues now saw him more as a prima donna.

After explaining he must reduce his work hours for his health's sake, we insisted he hire another experienced colorist to share the burden. Reluctantly he did so, but within a month that employee quit. Over the next year two others, all skilled technicians, departed. Though they certainly weren't of his caliber, they were competent. Rarely, however, did the new people satisfy his impossible standards. He claimed they were inept and interfered with his own amazing productivity.

As our growth continued, the demands on the lab had become so great, no matter how many hours our star technician worked, he could no longer keep up. Service declined. We agonized over the problem, torn between the recognition our perfectionist genius was one in a million and the undeniable fact he had now become a liability. Indeed, he was single-handedly holding down our progress.

The solution was to hire a knowledgeable, college-educated older man to head the lab as Technical Director. He didn't have the hands-on capabilities of the technician or his assistants but he was an experienced administrator. His responsibility was managerial and broader than our technician's. For instance, he scheduled customer requests and relieved the genius of dealing directly with customers on quality matters. He also provided the technical support for our sales staff.

We created a new layer to insulate the technician from the demands of running the lab. In doing this we hoped to utilize his true talent to its utmost. But it meant the genius, no longer his own boss, was now accountable to a specific individual whose office looked out on his bailiwick.

Having been warned well in advance this was coming and why, he seemed receptive to the idea. At last he could pursue his real love, the formulating of colors, without hindrance or distraction. Of course, his staff of assistants still reported to him.

At the outset all was good will and smiles. The genius produced formulations more accurate and breathtakingly swift than ever before. Some were works of art in their simplicity, a valuable quality because the simpler the formulation the less chance for error in production. Yet, after a couple of months, the lab's total output reverted to its former state of decline. We were baffled.

The lab's high employee turnover continued unabated. Why? The genius, overly critical of his assistants, caused them to quit in disgust. But the director had taken steps to correct the problem. Now he had every technician reporting directly to him, in effect stripping the genius of his authority and leaving him to his own devices.

At first, the genius accepted this state of affairs. He pursued his formulating, to the admiration of all, with a vengeance. The productivity of his assistants climbed. Lab output improved and our service capability resumed its former efficiency. Indeed, as the lab caught up with demand, no longer did the genius have to work day and night to keep up. This, it seemed, was intolerable to him.

Storming into my office, he demanded being placed in charge of the lab again. He issued an ultimatum: either I fire the Technical Director whom he branded as incompetent, or he would leave. Taking the rational approach, I pointed out the lab had never been in better shape. Since results are what count, I had no basis for meeting his demands. I realized reasoning would be in vain. The lab's very success and the fact his role was no longer crucial was at the root of the problem. Our genius recognized, as did everyone else, he was no longer indispensable. It was more than he could bear.

I told him he could leave. He was stunned but he left. During the next few months, as morale improved, lab output skyrocketed. Perhaps our formulations were less than the works of art we were used to, but they were adequate. Still, we were astonished our so called ordinary technicians were doing so well. At last they were at peace and free to grow to new heights.

Someone once said: give me two or three ordinary persons over a single genius. Our case amply illustrates that preference. Yet, were it not for our genius we probably wouldn't have made it at the beginning.

Who's on Top When?

Our company had just built an attractive new plant in the industrial park after three years of struggle. It told the world, at least outwardly, we were making it. Many vendors who had ignored us began knocking on our door. That included the president of the largest paper supply house in town. Bypassing our purchasing agent, he insisted on seeing me first.

I knew him well: he had fired me five years earlier when, as his office manager, I had an altercation with his son who was then the shipping clerk of his successful distribution and packaging firm. The son had gone through the mail on my desk before I had a chance to sort it and distribute it to the proper parties. After he had invaded my turf several times, I took a stand - and lost.

Now I was CEO and an owner of my own company. The father, wishing to supply all our paper and packaging needs, sought to make peace. He apologized for what had happened and said his son was no prize but he was sure I'd understand - a son's blood is thicker than an employee's.

This was the first time I had experienced the revival of an old and bitter relationship from the top. For years as an employee I played it safe and would quietly endure what I considered unfair treatment by my superiors. Whenever I felt compelled to assert myself, I would usually lose. It never occurred to me that one day I would have a chance at retribution.

As the paper company president sat before me giving his spiel, I recalled the old hurt. But it was irrelevant. My chance at retribution seemed empty. When I had worked for him, his prices had been quite competitive. I instructed our purchasing agent to do business with him strictly on the basis of price, quality and service. As it turned out, he came through much to our advantage.

Another instance in which an unpleasant relationship was awakened occurred when my former boss, the son of the president of a highly successful manufacturing company, wrote me seeking a job. Twenty years earlier I had been his employee as an expeditor and production scheduler. Rarely had I composed a schedule that suited him; rarely would he refrain from re-doing my work. I felt useless, redundant.

After a year he informed me I was no longer needed. Indeed, he never should have hired me in the first place.

His letter made no reference to our earlier fruitless relationship. Hearing our company was doing well, he extolled his managerial ability. But I knew his abilities precisely, or rather his deficiencies.

How did this man, now in his early 50s, having inherited his millionaire father's business, come to write such a letter? As CEO, he had borrowed heavily to expand his business which catered to a narrow market. When recession struck his market contracted, while overseas producers were overwhelming his domestic customers causing them to fail one by one. He made the mistake of the rich person who would invest all his wealth into one stock. Overloaded with debt, his once-thriving enterprise went bankrupt.

Though my memory of how he had demeaned my worth was still vivid, my reply letter turned him down gently. I felt no joy in doing so. Having fallen so far, he was in a pitiful way. Retribution, I discovered, is rarely sweet.

The most ironic revival of an old and soured relationship involved the large, closely held manufacturing corporation that bought my company. Thirty years earlier as its employee I had been the supervisor of a department responsible for inspecting one of its many products.

The company's research director, a brilliant (he held several patents) but difficult and arbitrary man, one day entered my department and ordered me to pass certain products I had classified as defective. I refused, stating I didn't agree with his judgement and suggested he clear his request through my boss, the production manager. Outraged, he ordered me to obey. If he said black was white, I had better agree. No way, I replied. He threatened to have me fired.

Within the hour the president of the company called me to his office. The research director was present. Perhaps I hadn't appreciated the RD's authority. It's essential I follow his instructions. Furthermore I must apologize. If I refused I was done. The RD had issued an ultimatum: it was either him or me. I chose to walk. Of course, this was before I had a non-working wife, children, and a mortgage.

Thirty years after this incident, the president, now chairman, hearing my company was for sale, sent his emissary to my office. After hammering out the better part of an agreement during several weeks of negotiation, the emissary and I deadlocked on one particular item. The chairman called and suggested he and I settle the matter over lunch. I marveled at how different that meeting was from the one we had so many years before. Neither of us referred to my dismissal. We resolved the sticky issue in three minutes and spent the rest of the lunch catching up on each other's personal history.

All went smoothly at the signing. When it was over and the lawyers and executives on both sides of the table rose to congratulate each other, I shook the chairman's hand and smiled. It would have cost him a lot less, I said, if he had never fired me. For a moment he stood puzzled, then as he remembered that final episode so long ago in his office, he beamed. "You're right," he said, "I shouldn't have done it." Who could have guessed?

There was so much joy in that moment of passing papers, that my moment of retribution was but an ironic joke, defused of any enmity. Life's twists are beyond imagining. No door to a relationship is ever completely shut.

Fitting the Job to the Person,
Not the Person to the Job

Business was good. I bought my wife a new Honda and attended a week long seminar in the Caribbean to learn about personality types, behavioral patterns and preferences. Until then I hadn't known only 10 percent of the population (thank God) possesses the right combination of characteristics to qualify as leaders. And I wasn't sure where I stood (Was I really suited to be CEO of my company?) until I answered a series of probing questions with supreme honesty. My wife, claiming the test was redundant, verified its accuracy. All I need have done was ask her, she said.

On the flight home, speculating on the implications of this new knowledge, and how I might apply it to my organization, I figured it would probably prove of little value. After all, weren't my employees the cream that rose to the top from the hundreds that sank on the job and became history over the years? Weren't they all relatively happy and doing what they do best?

Still, I wondered if a poll was taken asking any of us whether we are happy with our jobs, happy doing what we're doing, how many would say, yes?

Another question: among those who say they are happy, how many would say, given the choice, they would rather be doing something else? The significant phrase is "given the choice".

And a third question: how many are doing the kind of work for which they are constitutionally best suited?

My personal experience provided a clue. Though I had realized the American dream of succeeding in business by working hard and applying what natural entrepreneurial skills I possessed (despite feeling I was short on such talent), often I had the sense I would rather be doing something else. Frankly, although it took me a long time to come to it, I yearned to do work that allowed me more creative self-expression without having to be concerned with earning money, or, at any rate, lots of it. It turned out after a long business career, quite to my surprise, that success in business wasn't really my goal. At best it was only a means to it. I secretly dreamed of becoming a writer.

Who hasn't attended an elementary or high school reunion to find several of the class dunces, the so-called under-achievers, have grown up to become brilliant business leaders, respected politicians or another Einstein (a seeming dunce who had once failed math)? So the schools, not unlike my own company, have also been guilty of ignoring the special differences and talents among its "worker" students.

Who among us had underutilized or unrecognized capabilities and would seize the chance to use them given the opportunity? And how, assuming there was room for most of us to grow, could we discover those latent talents?

Fired up by the prospect of learning more about my employees and of offering each the opportunity to learn more about him or herself, I held an early Monday meeting with the administrative staff in the cafeteria and explained the test. To offer proof of its credibility, I showed them the results of my test. They all nodded vigorously - especially when I mentioned my tendency to control people.

By Friday, after most had volunteered and taken the personality profile quiz (there were a few holdouts initially), I felt like a prospector who had just struck gold.

Take Sylvia, a confident young woman with an outgoing nature and a twinkle in her eye. Her tasks included receiving incoming phone orders and processing the associated routine paper work. When we discussed her test results in the privacy of my office I asked whether she was happy with her job. Of course she was, she replied. But her profile showed a hidden aggressiveness; indeed she had a combination of qualities that would make an ideal salesperson.

Did she know this about herself? Of course she did, she answered with a knowing smile. Would she like to do inside selling, solicit business by phone, pave the way for our reps to call on prospective customers? It was a new sales approach for our company. She could hardly contain her enthusiasm. When could she start? She knew just what she wanted to do. I asked myself: was this real or fool's gold?

The word spread and everyone grew impatient for their interview.

Emma our office manager, a self-assured woman in her 50s, was a surprise in a different way.

The profile revealed her to be a "counselor" type. I asked what did she like most about her job. Her reply was not what I expected. What she prized doing was not what she was hired to do, nor what I had most valued in her work. Indeed, she said the most valuable service she rendered the company was her assumption of the role of ombudsman, a role most companies aren't lucky enough to have filled.

She was our pressure valve. Why hadn't I seen it? I recalled everyone went to her with their problems, not so much for solutions, but simply to be heard. And come to think of it, I too, in a subtle way, unloaded my complaints on her willing ears.

So I came to appreciate Emma and understand her true worth for the first time. I encouraged her to continue. She had created her own job, one that didn't appear on our job description list.

But Dennis, our technical director with a degree in chemistry, was our most momentous discovery. He ran our lab and oversaw quality control, a narrow kind of responsibility. The preferences revealed him to be an inspirational leader, a heavyweight in the Eisenhower mold. If ever an employee was underutilized, Dennis was. Did he realize he could take on considerably more responsibility? Well, yes he did, but he had no complaints. Before we hired him he was employed as an embalmer. He considered himself lucky to be out of that and to be our technical director.

Ah, but Dennis was, if I were to take the revelations seriously, capable of running the company if given the chance - capable of replacing me. And my profile showed a highly unbusiness side which I kept to myself. I liked solitude, to look inward. I liked to write.

What would Dennis think were I to groom him for the presidency? We'd take it slowly, of course, gradually phase him in. He didn't exactly say "Hallelujah," but it amounted to the same thing.

We began giving the test to job applicants and found ourselves doing counseling. We felt obligated to review the test with every applicant and to direct him or her where true talent and inclination lay. I felt it was the least we could do for the human race. Some were obviously not for us, but those that were according to the test results, usually made it.

Meanwhile, after a few months we had to give Sylvia an assistant to handle the routine work so she could devote full time to her sales effort. Occasionally she even joined the sales rep in the field, consolidating our position with the customer.

As for Dennis, he eventually took on the whole works. That I was able to complete my first novel with few distractions bears testimony to his capability.

[Postscript: The personality profile is based on Jung's theory of psychological types which are defined by individual differences in behavioral style and personal preferences. Some of us like olives and some of us don't. Some of us hate surprises and some of us find them exciting.

By the way, a psychologist recently informed me that such tests are illegal nowadays when given to job applicants. Too bad. They were beneficial to applicants by giving them a more fruitful direction to follow.]

The Manager Who Would Be His Own CEO

The manager of our Midwest plant was upset and on the phone. It was Friday morning and the pay checks hadn't arrived in the mail - the second time this had happened in a month. I suggested he write substitute checks from the company's limited local account established for just such emergencies.

This can't continue, he announced. Why do the people at headquarters discriminate against his facility? He recited a litany of injustices committed against his small organization. We had overcharged him for raw materials transferred from the mother plant to his. We had returned his reports for completion in which there were only minor omissions. He felt adrift, alienated. We were neglecting him.

I protested that none of what he was saying was true. We spoke daily; I visited him monthly. But his complaints contained a paranoid quality that worried me. I knew I had better fly out to see him immediately and talk things over.

Certainly the staff at headquarters had not been without complaints against him as well. They had found him demanding, uncooperative, often causing confusion by breaking procedural rules. At one point when relations between him and the staff had reached an impasse, we held a meeting with everyone involved at headquarters. Several misunderstandings were clarified and a new congeniality resulted. But now, just two months later, his antagonism had returned in a form more virulent than ever. Previously he had blamed the system, now he was accusing people of deliberate malice.

It was difficult to convince him his suspicions were unjustified. The people he dealt with at headquarters had nothing to gain by not cooperating with him. However, his complaint had some validity: his arrogance may well have promoted their badwill. I suggested he moderate his demands and be more tolerant of their occasional errors.

Most troubling to the organization, however, was his insistence at not conforming to our product formulations. We had purposely standardized the composition of all our custom-made products so we could produce the same product at either plant. This eliminated variation and assured our customers of the fastest possible service. Since both plants were rarely scheduled to capacity at the same time, we could generally guarantee availability at one facility or the other. But by substituting one ingredient for another, as our manager was prone to do, we could not provide our customer with what he expected.

In fairness, the manager's tampering with formulations was usually creative. His substitute ingredients were often cheaper or performed better than the existing ones. No one at headquarters disputed the argument his changes were improvements. But it was mandatory both facilities be in synch. I had stipulated that all concerned first approve any beneficial change before making it standard. This procedure would guarantee product uniformity.

Our manager rarely waited to share his innovations with the rest of the company. To my dismay he frequently delighted in one-upping his colleagues with changes that disturbed the peace. I urged him to strike a balance between being an iconoclast and a team player. I told him he must consider the larger purpose of the organization and its need for procedural structure and cooperation among its personnel. We were in this together, both our star performers and our average people.

He said he couldn't be happy under such circumstances. Such conformity would suffocate him. How could I deny him the opportunity to make things better? He needed a free hand. I should believe in him, allow him to take his operation down its own road.

I was torn between permitting a recognized talent to pursue ends that would most likely benefit the company, and restricting it for the sake of organizational harmony and operational smoothness. Perhaps, I also feared that were I to make him, in essence, his own CEO, the day would come when he would challenge my authority. Though a coup d'etat was hardly conceivable, a campaign for ever-increasing power certainly was.

I suggested he should be in his own business. So long as he worked for somebody he would be subject to their constraints. Of course, even on his own he would be constrained by bankers, customers and employees, but that was for him to discover. He said the idea had crossed his mind.

Several months later he quit and opened a facility similar to ours in the same community. He took with him our key lab technician, his brother (whom he had hired over my objection) and the facility's largest account in the area. But most troublesome were rumors he said he quit because of our mismanagement, and that we were a Jewish organization. (Of nearly 100 employees at the time, three were Jewish.)

His company thrived and, despite his attempts to damage us, so did ours. His appeals to customers' prejudice had backfired in many instances and had actually hurt his cause. His misrepresentation of the reasons for quitting eventually seemed spurious as our staying power proved. We had no regrets he left. As later events revealed he lacked the moral stature to which our organization aspired. What a pity he hadn't used his obvious abilities with dignity. A good bottom line simply isn't enough. How you arrive at it, is just as important. He had missed that point all along.

The Alcoholic Employee

Emil was the best machine operator we ever had. His hourly output surpassed that of any of his co-workers. But his total production for the year was the worst.

There were periods when he worked only a three or four day week. He had been ill, he would say, or he'd make some transparent excuse. We saw no pattern to his absences except that they occurred mostly after a weekend. During such times he was given to moods of surliness.

This went on for a couple of years. We endured him because he was such a superb worker. But eventually his foreman's patience wore thin. He warned Emil that the company could no longer tolerate his erratic attendance. A few days later Emil came to my office and announced he was an alcoholic. For the next month he worked a full five day week. He seemed proud of this achievement. Then he didn't show up for several days. The foreman hesitated to take action. How could he fire his best worker? My opinion was sought. Let him go, I counseled. He was too disruptive.

This was my first encounter with alcoholism in our company. Our dilemma with Emil required us to more clearly define the company's responsibility to its employees. When do personal problems become company problems? How far should the company go in dealing with an employee's problem? Certainly bottom line considerations are important, but so are human considerations. We were small enough so that every individual was important. Management felt that while the company expected an employee's loyalty, the employee deserved the company's loyalty in return. With that in mind, we reached out to Emil as best we could.

Before we let him go, we gave him fair warning. Unless we could depend on him and unless he would adopt a more cooperative spirit, he was at risk of dismissal. But losing him was painful because he performed his job so well. It was also painful to see his talent wasted and his debilitating problem unresolved.

Soon after, we were tested again. This time the problem involved an executive, our production vice-president, who had joined us in his late twenties as a shift supervisor. Roger was bright, dedicated and had won everyone's respect. For ten years he had performed every task he was assigned like a champion. Indeed, he designed the incentive system which saved our company from certain disaster. But unfortunately the foundation of our relationship held some hidden cracks.

Roger strode into my office one morning, appearing disheveled, and demanded an outrageous increase in salary. It was an act totally out of character. Year after year his wages had climbed handsomely, making him one of the highest paid employees in the company. In the course of our discussion he revealed his wife felt he was underpaid. Unless he earned more she would leave him. Do wives customarily leave husbands for such a reason? This scenario struck me as strange. I refused to meet his demand and asked that he reconsider. After all, we had had a long and fruitful relationship and his future with us was assured.

The next morning he returned to my office and confessed he was an alcoholic. His marriage, he said, was "going to the dogs." Suddenly I understood why he had totalled a company car only a few weeks earlier, why he walked around with a Coke in his hand all day, and why he had made a spate of judgement errors in recent months.

Having suffered the loss of one good man to alcohol, I wanted very much to salvage this one if possible. The fact that Roger had come clean was a good sign. But I was leery of keeping him in charge of production. Some of his errors had been costly.

Roger said he had just joined Alcoholics Anonymous. He handed me an AA pamphlet to read to help me understand the organization's methods. He wished to leave the area and leave his family while he put himself back together. I suggested a possible solution: We had an opening for a salesman in the southeast, a virgin territory for us. We'd maintain his salary until sales developed and provide him a car and expense account. With his knowledge of our product, his processing expertise and keen imagination, he would be invaluable to prospective customers. Without a moment's hesitation he accepted. But I imposed one condition: that he attend an AA meeting every day no matter where he was. He willingly agreed.

Roger took up jogging and became healthy. For almost two years he adhered to our agreement, building the territory into one of our best. Then on his second Christmas he came north to visit his family and make peace. He told me he wished to return and rebuild his life. Of course we had replaced him with his very competent assistant. There was no other opening. Roger then admitted he wished to move on, anyway. Twelve years with the same company was long enough. From his point of view, I couldn't disagree. We kept him on while he searched for another job. He found one as production manager of a plant three times our size. Had we lost a good employee the second time? Not really. Our friendly relationship continued. Often he'd drop by for a visit. After all, the bottom line isn't everything.

Compensating Salesmen in the Real World

We had two classes of sales people: those who earned too little and those who earned too much.

The first were on straight salary, and the company provided them with a car, paid their expenses and awarded them automatic raises annually. They religiously called on the same accepting customers week after week. But they approached new prospects with less fervor and, if after some months they received only scant encouragement, their call frequency declined. It wasn't that these salesmen weren't motivated - they coveted success; rather it was that after a year or two they tended to slide into a comfortable rut as did their sales volume.

The second types were independent representatives (reps). They were fanatics working day and night for a straight 5 percent commission wooing the biggest customers and securing the biggest orders. Their relationship with their (not our) customers seemed almost blood-based. Since we couldn't be sure of their customer's loyalty, regardless of our product or service, we never felt secure. The rep, knowing this, often made unreasonable demands on us and he usually got away with it. After all, losing a rep meant more than simply losing a sales person.

The business the reps brought in was usually more profitable to them than to the company. While they were sure of their 5 percent, the company wasn't always sure of making a profit. Indeed, the reps relished the marginal big volume business which enhanced their dollar sales and their commissions without regard for the company. Our common interest was limited.

A dream salesman would be one who combined a rep's entrepreneurial drive with a loyal employee's dedication. To put it in practical terms, such a salesman would require considerable autonomy and the capacity to earn increasing income consistent with the company's bottom line.

It was time to take a hard look at the way things really were, not at the way we always assumed they were.

We had assumed:

*A salesman cannot be expected to secure 100 percent of the business in his territory.

*A salesman must not be allowed to earn more than his boss.

*A salesman must not know what a product costs to produce, or what it contributes to the bottom line.

*A salesman must confine his role strictly to selling, not to other matters concerning the company.

Then we reversed our assumptions.

*Every salesman must know the company's concerns, spend at least two or three days each quarter attending management meetings and touring the plant, speaking with the workers, the foremen, the supervisors, and our lab and office personnel. He must have a sense of the organization behind him and of his oneness with it.

*If our price for an item proves uncompetitive the salesman must be advised of its cost, of the minimum profit we seek, and given authority to requote if possible.

But our compensation system would make the big difference.

*Expect the salesman to capture every account in his territory. As it becomes more and more difficult to do so, reward him accordingly. After all, the more business he writes the more difficult it becomes to secure additional business. Each new customer creates a diminishing number of prospects, usually those most resistant to changing suppliers.

We told our salesmen: the company will provide you with a car, expenses and a base salary to take care of your family's basic needs. But from your first sales dollar on, you will receive a commission at an INCREASING RATE as your sales climb. There is no limit to your income and your territory is sacrosanct. Let's see what you can do.

*The rate of commission increased according to a fixed schedule with each $100,000 increment of sales. Were a salesman to achieve a maximum (and feasible) sales level for his territory he would conceivably earn more than his sales manager whose income was tied to profitability and not sales. Sales don't necessarily result in profits.

However, it was calculated realistically so his income would not exceed that which the company would pay a commissioned rep. Yet, to our surprise and delight, one salesman surpassed that expectation.

*All salesmen, (as well as all other employees) would become shareholders at no cost, which would encourage them to be bottom line oriented. This was a weaker, and obviously less direct, motivating force than the increasing commission rate.

As we hoped, each salesman's sales steadily increased, as did his monthly income. While he strove to reach the next higher commission level month after month throughout the year the reward grew sweeter and sweeter. Since income was tied to sales, the system automatically adjusted for inflation as our prices rose. That continued until the first oil embargo hit and inflation got out of hand. To keep pace with the depreciating value of money we increased the salesman's base salary.

The system ran smoothly for years - until a young, new salesman, after being on the road for a year, complained it was taking too long to attain the income level he felt he deserved. We failed to convince him our system required patience and tied reward directly to performance, and he quit. We knew then our compensation plan was alive and well and doing what it was supposed to do.

Lead Us Not into Temptation

As a young man starting out in plastic materials sales, I believed my job would be a cinch. After all, I represented a reputable company offering a superior product for less money than most of our competition. I assumed my success was logical and assured based on the way the marketplace was supposed to work.

But market logic, I soon learned, is only a general theory. In the college economics course I took they never taught the special theory: when a buyer's personal self-interest supersedes a company's interest, the general theory no longer applies. And I found more buyers in the field who subscribed to the special theory than I thought possible.

When a salesman enters a territory for the first time, he gropes to discover what would motivate each prospective customer to buy from him. Though he may have a dossier of statistical information on the customer, it is of marginal use as an aid. In fact, and more importantly, he's blind to the customer's prejudices, style, operational politics, and his deepest needs, all of which serve to counteract general market theory.

Why, I wondered, despite my most dedicated attention to certain prospective customers who clearly would save money by buying from me, did I so often fail to secure their business? Determined that market logic would ultimately prevail, I called on such accounts for years. Had I known the truth, I would have realized my efforts were futile.

The dawn broke for me in the case of XYZ company, presently America's largest corporation in its field. We had been doing substantial business with the company until the department head with whom we had been dealing quit. After he left, his department merged with another, run by an individual who I knew from first-hand experience was on the take. (Some years earlier when I managed a plastics molding plant, my employer was kicking back to this manager a percentage for every hour of contracted machine time spent producing for his company.) It was common knowledge among suppliers that to secure and retain his business it was necessary to provide him with expensive household gifts, paid vacations in the islands and sex. Since we wouldn't comply with such terms, his orders soon ceased.

Our representative, having successfully nurtured the account for several years, was understandably distraught over his loss of business. And our company sorely missed the orders which were often a mainstay during slow times. Even our workers in the plant were concerned. In desperation, our salesman, always an honorable man, suggested we go part way in meeting the customer's demands. As a matter of principle, and also from a prior distasteful experience with another company that indulged in payola, I refused. Where does such a thing end? No, we must stick with our policy of selling our products and services strictly according to their merits. It's the morally correct thing to do. If it means sacrificing a certain amount of business, so be it. But he rejected my proclamation as being rigid and self-righteous. The loss was too high for the small price we would have to pay. Wasn't everyone else doing it?

While our man had no choice but to follow the stricture I imposed, he was hurting where it hurts most: in the pocketbook. Feeling duty-bound to devise a remedy, I agreed to confront the customer's management with the truth. Ordinarily this would be a risky tactic; it could backfire and cost us the account for all time. After all, what did we know of the political layout within the company? Who had what vested interest in what was happening? And dishonesty aside, how profound was the relationship between the perpetrator and top management? Still, feeling we could lose no more than we had already, we took the chance.

I phoned the executive vice president, number two in command, and explained that having lost their business after many mutually beneficial years we were frustrated in our attempts to regain it. We would like to meet with him to get at the bottom of the problem. He agreed and we met in a couple of weeks - he saw no urgency.

After praising us for having serviced his company well, he said he had learned our competitors had under-priced us. How was that possible, we asked, since we had been denied the opportunity to submit current quotes. At this he picked up his phone and requested the department manager report to his office. Uncomfortable though we were, it seemed fair to us the manager should face his accuser. After he entered, and during the entire three-way conversation that followed, never did his eyes meet ours.

The manager asserted he was buying at the lowest possible price from current sources. Immediately I presented a list of our latest prices for the various materials his company had purchased from us in the past. Let's compare these with what you're now paying, I challenged. Our list was stacked: I had intentionally submitted prices that were below cost as a loss leader. This would also test the manager's truthfulness.

After examining the list, the manager reiterated the prices he was paying were the same as or below ours. I asked to see our competitors' invoices. The executive V.P. stiffened. To reveal such prices was contrary to company policy, he said. Furthermore, if the manager said it was so, that was good enough for him. We had lost. The issue had died in less than 15 minutes. Not surprisingly, we never did business with the company again.

At our next sales meeting, I elucidated our policy for dealing with buyers who sought favors. As CEO I couldn't live with any buyer/vendor relationship that compromised the well-being of the buyer's employer. Any favor we granted was bound to cost the employer sooner or later.

We would confine our favors only to taking buyers (and their spouses) out for lunch or dinner. Admittedly this would eliminate several major prospective accounts but hadn't we avoided dealing with credit risks - most often companies of doubtful morality who don't deal up front? Why not also discriminate on moral grounds against those who insist on dealing under the table? Isn't our self-respect

just as important to our organization as profits? Most of us -
but not all, I realized - could now live more comfortably with
ourselves. After all, we never expected to capture more than
a share of the market, anyway.

Who Needs the Customer Anyway?

Maine, Wednesday. The tenant calls to tell me
Hurricane Bob had blown down 12 trees and damaged a
stone wall on the grounds of my house on Cape Cod. Am I
insured?

Thursday. The receptionist at the insurance agent's
office on the Cape says the person I wish to talk to isn't at
her desk. Donna would return my call. Most of the day
passes. I call again. This time Donna is at a meeting; due to
the storm they are extremely busy. I plan to drive the 250
miles to the Cape over the weekend to view the damage.
Could I make an appointment to see Donna on Monday? No
appointments. It's first come first served.

I'm now feeling less than friendly. I merely want to
know whether I'm covered for wind damage. If I don't hear
from Donna on Friday, I'll be at her office Monday morning.
OK, sir. I'll tell her.

Maine, Friday. Silence.

Cape Cod, Monday A.M. The devastation is
shocking. I phone Donna. She's busy with a customer. Could
I make an appointment? No appointments. But I've traveled
250 miles for the purpose of settling this matter and I'm
returning to Maine that day. I must talk to her. We have
hundreds of other customers, sir. This pushes my outrage
button. How many have come my distance? I don't care
about your other customers. I'm sorry, sir. It's first come
first serve.

I'm irate. Though I believe in democracy and being equal, when it comes to being someone's customer, I wish to be king.

Two minutes later. I have the president of the agency on the line. He tells me I'm probably not insured. Has he seen the policy? He'll get back to me. Phoning later, he confirms my insurance doesn't cover the loss of trees. Donna tried to reach me in Maine, he says. Not before I left on Sunday, I say. Furthermore I have an answering machine. Well, you've got to understand we have over 1,000 customers, he answers. What do you know? As goes the receptionist, so goes the president, or rather, no doubt the reverse has happened.

With that statement, he pushes my outrage button so hard it gets stuck. For the past 16 years, with negligible claims, I had given this agent all my insurance business on cars, houses, boats, and umbrella.

Maine, Wednesday. My insurance policy expires in less than two weeks. I call another, smaller agency on the Cape whom a friend raved about for the service they provided after the storm. They now have my business - that is unless and until they tell me they have hundreds of other customers.

Years ago when I was a young 50-year-old CEO attending the Smaller Company Management Program (SCMP) at Harvard, one lesson I learned there affected my business outlook profoundly.

Early one morning 100 of us, all top company executives, gathered in an amphitheatre for a class in marketing. The professor opened the class by asking several of us, one by one, what we sold in our respective businesses. One president said he sold hot air balloons, another, advertising; another, newspapers; another, myself, plastic coloring materials and so on.

Baloney, boomed the professor. We were startled. Those were only the products we made and the services we provided. How could we be so blind? He laid it on heavy. As top dogs in our companies how could we not know what a sale consisted of?

One hundred company top executives were completely baffled. What we sold, said the professor, were relationships, and we'd better not forget it. I haven't.

I returned to my company fired up with this simple concept. First, we did little things. From then on, no customer who called would be told the party he or she wished to talk to was at a meeting. Customer's calls would be returned within two hours. In the event our person couldn't be reached within that time, someone else from the company contacted the customer to explain the delay and convey a message.

And we did big things. We would approach all customer complaints with an open mind. Complaints would receive top priority, attended to within hours, and be settled promptly. Rather than a negative experience, we viewed a complaint as an opportunity to prove our dependability and our concern for the customer's welfare.

Placing the idea of "selling a relationship" before the traditional one of selling a product, we humanized our approach. The cornerstone of building any relationship is familiarity. And how does one achieve that? Call frequency, of course. We mandated each of our salesmen visit every customer a minimum of once every two weeks - unless the customer objected, a rare instance.

Instructing our salesmen to never discuss our other customers (nor our competitors), we encouraged them to give the customer the impression our company had only one customer: them. And that our entire organization was dedicated to their cause. How did we confirm this? Our CEO made an appearance at their door at least once a year, had lunch with their CEO or purchasing agent or whoever called the shots.

Despite all our best efforts, we occasionally lost a customer, but we knew it and would ask why. I'll give odds the president of my former insurance agency has no idea he's lost me. Anybody out there willing to take me up on it?

Selling a Relationship, Not a Product or Service - A General Approach

*Salespeople will attend a training program in marketing and take refresher courses annually.

*Salespeople will attend a training program, preferably at the factory, on how the products he or she sells are made.

*Salespeople will be given detailed instructions on each feature of a product and shown its advantages and be tested on the information given.

*Salespeople will work in teams, if within a single location or territory the members assist each other.

*Salespeople will be multi-skilled, trained in all aspects of sales: product information, order taking, and solving of buyer's problems. An individual salesman will conduct the sale in all its phases from inception to completion.

*Salespeople will meet regularly (daily or weekly or monthly whichever is practical) to discuss strategy, and tactics in their respective bailiwicks.

*Salespeople will meet for a day each month to discuss problems (their failures) and seek solutions by means of "The Five Why's". Ask "Why" a sale was lost, for instance, five times. This forces the searcher to get nearer to the truth until the root cause of the problem is revealed. This method for discovering the truth was devised by the Japanese.

*Salespeople will regularly maintain a link with the customer and keep him informed, via phone or direct visits before, during and after a sale is made. Each salesman will become the customer's personal representative forever.

*Salespeople will learn what best suits the customer's needs, not his company's, and sell only the product or service that fits those needs.

*Salespeople (in the case of automobiles and capital goods) will see the product through preparation, help the customer register the vehicle (if applicable), and provide the customer an item by item rundown on each feature.

*Salespeople will be the customer's contact for maintenance (in the case of capital goods). In collaboration with the maintenance manager they will do the scheduling.

*Prices will be competitive and rigidly held in most instances.

*Commissions will be divided among the team members based on the number of days each salesperson worked.

*Each salesperson will receive a base salary which will increase with each year of service.

*At least once a quarter there will be a company-wide meeting in which the company's status, its problems and strategy are discussed. Again the Five Why's.

Experiments with Time

For 10 years before it was sold, our company was virtually a management laboratory. This is an account of three experiments. One failed, one was partially successful and one worked. The first was to eliminate the time cards of hourly paid workers.

In our view, punching in and out was demeaning, an assault on the dignity of the worker. But it was a convenient, time proven way for management to keep track of a worker's hours, especially overtime.

Since our manufacturing process which ran for two or, at times, three shifts per day involved machinery that couldn't be shut down without substantial startup cost, absenteeism and tardiness could be troublesome. For this reason we had a firm rule that the worker notify the shift leader in advance of any anticipated tardiness or absence so steps could be taken to fill the gap.

At a plant-wide meeting the workers enthusiastically approved management's proposal to abandon time cards. They would essentially become salaried and be on their honor to submit correct hours for overtime compensation. They would also be responsible for policing themselves with respect to absenteeism and tardiness.

For several months the experiment went smoothly - even making it easier for the payroll staff to compute each worker's weekly compensation. But soon the daily production report showed an occasional drop-off which prompted an investigation. We traced several such occasions to late machinery start-up times or to equipment remaining idle while awaiting the arrival of a tardy second shift person.

At the next quarterly plant-wide meeting in which we reviewed the P & L statement and discussed the company's problems, we confronted the issue. Without mentioning suspects, we pointed out the tardiness of a few had adversely affected output and it was up to the production crew to do something about it.

During the next quarter, tardiness, though reduced, persisted. We called another meeting specifically to deal with the matter. Our frustration was mutual: neither management nor workers could come up with a solution short of firing the guilty parties. No one wished to do so. Reluctantly we reinstated the time cards.

Only after introducing a team incentive system years later, did we find time cards superfluous. When money was involved the workers were motivated sufficiently to discipline themselves and each other.

Around that time, the four-day work week was becoming the rage. With our penchant for introducing new management techniques, we asked our workers whether they'd be interested. Both our plants (in the northeast and the Midwest) voted unanimously to try it. Half the crews worked 10 hours a day from Monday to Thursday and the other half from Tuesday to Friday. Management and support staff worked a standard five-day week.

This arrangement gave the worker longer weekends for leisure, and provided the company more opportunity to schedule overtime when necessary. We found the workers more willing to work overtime on a fifth day (a Monday or Friday), or part of one, than to work on a Saturday under the old five-day schedule. The difference, of course, was the four-day week allowed the weekend to remain intact regardless of overtime. We detected no significant difference in either output or morale.

After three months, a vote was held on whether to continue the four-day week schedule. To our surprise, the northeast plant, consisting of mostly older workers, voted to return to the standard five-day week, while the Midwest plant, comprised of principally younger workers, wished to retain the four-day schedule. Perhaps the older workers found the 10 hour day too strenuous - though no one had ever complained except on an exceptionally hot summer day. Or were they just bound to an old habit? Since both facilities ran independently, each was allowed to follow the schedule of choice.

In any case, based on this experience we were inspired to tinker with time in another way.

Flexible time also being the rage, the office was the perfect place to try it - at least our homegrown version. By unanimous consent the staff agreed to the following:

*Everyone must work 40 hours per week.

*An employee must report to work no later than 10 A.M. nor quit any earlier than 3 P.M.

*Every employee must learn how to perform his or her co-workers' tasks.

*In order to arrive late or leave early, an employee must arrange for a substitute person to cover the hours he or she is absent.

How did it work? Famously.

The employees, especially mothers, were freed to be with their children more, to keep doctors' appointments without losing work time, and to go shopping without crowds. On Fridays, it gave them a slightly longer weekend.

As for our managers, besides enjoying a happier environment, they were startled to see office workers reporting to work as early as 7 A.M. which, before the phones began ringing at 9 o'clock, gave them an unexpectedly efficient use of two uninterrupted hours.

There was, however, one minor point of confusion. When expecting a particular person to furnish specific information and/or to perform a task, management suddenly found that person might be out of the office. Who then must one call on to get something done? This forced our poor executives to funnel all requests through the office manager, a procedure they should have followed all along. So, even though our managers had trouble getting the hang of it, much to the amusement of the office staff, flexible time remained in effect indefinitely.

Beware, Friends and Relatives at Work

When you're on top it's natural to want to help those hitting bottom. Thus, on three separate occasions during my tenure as CEO, I came to the aid of a friend and two relatives by hiring them. In each instance, sooner or later I had to fire them. Obviously I was hard put to learn the lesson: Never hire souls with whom you have a relationship that you value.

When my wife's cousin's husband failed in business at an age - his early 50s - that few firms find investment-grade, I took a chance. He was personable if somewhat laid back, with a sales background suitable for the slot I was about to fill in our young company. Furthermore, I believed a mature individual who had suffered hard knocks would be more stable, more dedicated, and more appreciative of an opportunity than an ambitious younger candidate who might expect to rise to the top almost overnight.

For more than 10 years this thesis proved correct. To provide encouragement at the beginning, I assigned him our largest account, one I opened only a year earlier. With his positive spirit and hard work, he eventually developed a loyal cadre of customers which earned him more income than he had ever dreamed. Both he and his wife expressed their gratitude in numerous ways, including invitations to social gatherings and family weddings and weekends on an island. Often I congratulated myself. His employment certainly appeared to be a truly serendipitous move.

In the eighth year he lost his two major accounts, (including the one I had delegated to him). It had a devastating effect on our sales and his income. His employment was under no threat, since the causes of the losses were extraneous to his efforts. But the pressure was on to replace the lost business; this involved expanding his territory into the tough metropolitan New York market. At his age, early 60s, he hardly viewed this as the promised land. (A younger man would probably have begged for the larger market.)

Though our sales manager, his boss, explained the need for new accounts - even revealing our precarious bottom line - he failed to respond. Instead, preferring to socialize with his tried and true customers, he resumed his tired old itinerary. After the third reminder he must do more, we realized he had no intention of complying. At his stage of life, he pointed out, he wished to stick with a comfortable pace and eventually ease off.

Who could blame him? But this hardly satisfied the company's need for extra effort to help keep us in the black. Our sales manager, agonizing over the "blood" relationship, wished to fire him. Also agonizing, I proposed that he be made an independent rep, retaining the core of his regular accounts whom he could call on as he saw fit. No longer under pressure to perform, he could be assured of an income in proportion to whatever effort he wished to apply. I saw it as a way that would allow him to gradually ease into retirement. At the same time, it freed the company to hire a salesperson who could actively pursue added business both in his and the expanded territory.

Unfortunately he saw this suggestion as an act of betrayal. After all, he said, didn't the company owe him for securing (false) and servicing (true, for which he was compensated) its largest account (since lost) for almost a decade? For his 10 years of service wasn't it the company's responsibility to maintain him until he retired? When we refused, he quit and found a job with a competitor calling on the very accounts we had offered him - at even less income. As a result, for years he and his family boycotted me and mine. The rift, at least between his family and me, will always remain.

The second case concerned a friend and once good customer who had lost his administrative job when his company was sold. Feeling we knew his abilities well, we hired him as our office manager. After six months he proved to be a non-producer who constantly equivocated and got bogged down in detail so things simply didn't get done. The job was not the right one for him.

Following several warnings he grew distraught. His performance worsened. We had no choice but to fire him, and much bitterness resulted. It only deepened when our new manager advised the state's unemployment office he had been dismissed for ineptitude, thus foreclosing his opportunity to collect. I had lost forever a friend whom I had liked and respected.

The third case, the son of another cousin of my wife's, caused me enormous personal grief because he was a winning young man who held great promise. Bright, imaginative, a self-starter and confident, he had the qualities of a charismatic leader. I was secretly grooming him to be my replacement when I would retire four or five years hence.

For two years we trained him from the bottom, exposing him to all phases of our manufacturing and development procedures. His success in each instance only confirmed our confidence in his abilities. We assigned him to sales, first as a trainee, later to his own territory for an anticipated three-year stint. This would be his last stepping stone to a high administrative position.

But in the third year he complained his compensation as a salesman, which was comparable to that of his colleagues, was insufficient. He had to compromise his standard of living, he said, which required that his in-laws and parents subsidize him. He had earned considerably more when he worked for his father's large publicly-held corporation - a non-job which bored him and from which he had been dismissed.

During repeated lunches, I appealed to his patience, explaining that under our compensation plan, he would inevitably increase his income as his sales increased. I further pointed out it would have an adverse effect on the morale of our entire sales force were I to play favorites. I hinted that as he mastered his responsibilities bigger and better things would be open to him in the future. But most important of all, by building a territory through hard work, he would derive a sense of achievement, of receiving reward that was well earned, and of gaining a new level of self-respect.

Unfortunately I had been talking into the wind. By accident we discovered he had been spending much of his time, not selling, but at home or assisting friends who had recently opened an upscale restaurant. He had faked his itinerary on the weekly call reports and had used the company's credit card to make personal phone calls across the country. Too bad, he had it all, except an understanding that the means to success is more important than success itself. Of course, we quickly ended our relationship.

The failure in each case cannot be attributed to the prior connection. It could just as well have happened with strangers. Would I have hired these people without their connection? Perhaps, perhaps not. Clearly, the price of failure was much higher than if strangers were involved. The company lost, but the employee and I lost much more - a valued relationship that will never be rekindled. When my brother and sister-in-law suggested I employ their son who had just graduated college, I had no trouble refusing. Their love and friendship were far too precious to risk losing.

Sex and the CEO

When an employee is distracted by harassment from the boss, both they and the enterprise are bound to suffer from the inefficiencies that result. The energy expended is enormous and better applied to the business. But what about those relationships that flower into successful sexual liaisons? Are these, the precise opposite of harassment, of benefit to the enterprise?

As a CEO who has experienced such a relationship, I categorically submit the answer is NO. What follows is necessarily from a male's point of view. But I suspect a female CEO would encounter similar consequences were she to establish a sexual relationship with a junior executive.

Usually the CEO and his employee paramour try to keep their business with each other businesslike. Their functions demand it, but more important, they behave in this manner because they don't want the rest of the company to know. They spend much effort creating diversions necessary to maintain secrecy. Of course they have no idea the rest of the company already knows, has known by the time they had their second date. None of this helps them perform on the job, or for that matter, improves the performance of the other employees as they gossip about the affair during worktime.

Unless the CEO is so smitten he's lost all judgement - an unlikely scenario - it remains that he must keep his eye on his main purpose: the welfare and success of the company. But the object of his affection, although well aware of his position and responsibility (indeed, perhaps they are his main attraction), finds it difficult to separate the man who is her leader from the man who is her lover. This leads to a disastrous misunderstanding: she thinks he values her welfare above that of the company - or should; he thinks she realizes the company must come first.

When I first became aware of this difference in priorities, I appointed a third party, a middle level executive, above my friend to insulate us from each other while at work. Though at first she objected, I convinced her it would make working conditions more comfortable and could only improve our intimate relationship. Though CEOs tend to be effective manipulators, we aren't as good at controlling events as we think. Unwittingly, I had set the scene for an explosion.

After a number of weeks she came to my office - a practice I thought had ended - to report her superior had asked her to change certain procedures I had established. I reminded her he was her boss. She must do things the way he wanted them done. She saw his insistence as a betrayal, as disloyalty to me. I indicated I had no objection. She expressed outrage. In her view my agreeableness was a surrender of power. I insisted she do as her boss directed and the issue was really not my concern.

At the time I failed to understand what was happening. Looking back, I now realize she resented the distance I had created between us, that changing the old procedure confirmed its finality. But who had time while in the throes of managing a bustling company to speculate on the inner needs and desires of an emotional employee? Obviously I should have put aside my compulsion to tend to business and taken the time. She was, after all, more than just an employee. But business must come first, right?

In short order she returned to my office with an ultimatum, an approach that in my experience never works. If I wouldn't reinstate the old procedure, the one she was used to, then she would have to quit. I tried reasoning with her, explaining that to undermine her boss's authority would have undesirable repercussions. Uncertain of my loyalty and devotion, she was testing me. But I could never waver from the belief one's job and one's personal life are best kept apart. In the workplace the company must win. I told her she could quit if there was no other way. She left the office, never to return.

So my involvement cost us the loss of an outstanding employee, who, by the way, we had trouble replacing for some time. After her departure, I came to realize how stressful our affair had been. Suddenly, no longer needing to hide anything, I felt less constrained in dealing with my immediate staff. I even sensed a subtle relief among them, a more relaxed attitude toward me. But most surprising, the affair, rather than ending, actually blossomed as both she and I found ourselves more at ease with each other. No longer did the company come between us. And in not seeing each other throughout the day, we found our less frequent contact with each other sweeter.

To have an affair in business is a needless and demanding complication. Be warned: any employee who becomes emotionally involved with the boss does so at great risk. And I urge every CEO to carry a bumper sticker: Love and business don't mix.

CHAPTER III

THE BUYOUT

A Banker's Faith

After a string of good years, we were now 100 souls in the midst of the oil embargo. The phone had virtually stopped ringing; each month our P & L showed accumulating losses. My equal partner (he was treasurer and I was president), was convinced the situation was temporary. After all, the plastics industry for which we manufactured color concentrates had grown year after year and always faster than the economy. By reading economic reports I believed we were in for a lengthy recession. This time the plastics industry would not be spared.

My partner and I had been at odds over this for some time. Policy was at a stalemate. We agreed we had to divorce; one of us had to buy out the other.

Price was a given because we had established the value of the company in writing every year in case either one of us died. Since he had other businesses and sources of income and I depended solely on the company for mine (it comprised my total wealth), we agreed I would be the buyer. However, I had no personal financial resources nor any assurance of raising funds. But I believed, almost mystically, that I'd succeed.

I began with the banks - and ultimately approached five. They weren't interested. After all, were they to lend me what I needed, my balance sheet would show a negative net worth of $215,000 and combined debt of $1,439,000. Even our own bank, with whom we had had a long and salutary relationship, would not help.

I tried other possible sources: insurance companies, Small Business Investment Corporations (SBIC's), private investors and companies in related fields. Some were willing provided they took control. I would simply be swapping one partner for another. Worse still, I'd even lose my veto power. The buyout had to be an opportunity to captain my own ship. Not being in control was tantamount to slow death.

After six months of searching (amid mounting losses), having exhausted the market of available lenders and investors, I became discouraged. What I most dreaded was about to happen - it was my wealthy partner's turn to buy me out.

Then a remarkable and, at the time, innovative concept was casually mentioned by our pension plan consultant. (We opted against a pension plan that committed us to annual contributions. Instead we had a profit sharing plan that allowed us to make contributions arbitrarily.) Would I object to the employees doing the buyout? Object? Why, I would desire it. Who would make better partners than my employees? Our goals would be the same. But how? Where would they get the money?

Through an Employee Stock Ownership Plan (ESOP), the consultant said.

Only one company in the state had an ESOP then and less than a hundred existed in the nation. It was too early to know how well they were working. Nevertheless here was a way to fund the buyout with pre-tax earnings: under the plan the company would be allowed to deduct 15 percent of its gross payroll from the bottom line, (thus reducing its tax) and pour it into an employee trust which in turn would purchase company stock (my partner's). Each employee would own stock in proportion to his or her wage. Since the tax rate then was 50 percent, in essence the trust would achieve the buyout with 50-cent dollars.

But there were some hitches depending on your point of view. Under the plan, the move necessitated revealing everything to the employees, particularly financial statements. They would also be allowed to vote for the company's officers and board members. Theoretically, if they considered me an incompetent president, they could throw me out.

My entrepreneur friends, owners of their own closely held companies, warned me that giving such powers to the employees would be dangerous and deprive me of all sorts of perks. I would no longer have autonomy. Secrecy is essential to control. A business is an autocracy. Democracy in management doesn't work.

What did I have to hide? What would happen if everyone knew where every cent went, knew the bottom line? If as owners the employees would benefit from our profits, they would also share my worry over our losses. Since I rarely took advantage of the perks available, I wouldn't miss them. After all, the ESOP, owning less than 50 percent of the stock, would give me control - a far more valuable benefit than any perk. And who knows, employee ownership might encourage a loyalty and dedication that would improve the bottom line. Wasn't it the U.S. Congress's idealistic belief that employee ownership would lead to a more equitable distribution of wealth and less strife between management and labor? (Another subject.)

If, based on the company's history, I could show realistic cash flow projections sufficient to fund the buyout, would our bank go along? Certainly, the bank replied, but our historical cash generation wouldn't justify their willingness. Ah, but if it were possible to use pre-tax dollars the cash flow would be there. Agreed, but that wasn't possible. I'd establish an ESOP and make it possible. What's an ESOP, the bank asked? From that moment our banker listened in rapt fascination as I explained how it would work. It was the bank's first encounter with the concept. Intrigued, they went for the deal I had negotiated with my partner.

Our lawyers hammered out an agreement to the satisfaction of my partner, the bank and myself. But the bank still had to live with the fact the company's debt exceeded its assets for an indeterminate length of time. After the signing at the bank, as we were driving back to the plant, my lawyer expressed wonderment that the bank had gone along. Yes, I said, it was incredible. Their faith in me must have been enormous, he said. Though the company went on to become highly successful, I have never felt more triumphant than on that day.

What's Wrong with an ESOP

A couple living together may think they know each other, but the true test of compatibility arrives only after marriage. Similarly, only after my closely held company married an ESOP (Employee Stock Ownership Plan) did I learn what I, as CEO and principal stockholder, had gotten myself into.

Would I, in retrospect, do it over again? Perhaps I'll find the answer by the end of this chapter. First, a little history. The Plan served its primary purpose well: to buy out a hostile partner's 50 percent share. Before considering an ESOP I tried raising capital from a range of sources: banks both large and small, SBIC's, insurance companies, private individuals, you name it. Lenders turned us down because we would necessarily show a negative net worth as a consequence of a loan. And we turned down investors because in every case they wished to control.

But when we hit upon the idea of an ESOP, thereby allowing the company to essentially pay off debt with tax deductible dollars (As I've indicated, we were in a 50 percent tax bracket at that time.), our regular bank hardly hesitated. Though our net worth was negative, current and projected cash flows were such that we could easily finance an annual contribution to the ESOP which in turn purchased, in prescribed installments, the ex-partner's stock held in escrow by the bank.

To review how our ESOP worked - the law permitted the company to contribute up to 15 percent of its gross annual payroll from profits to an Employee Trust (ESOT) (which, by the way, could also borrow, usually guaranteed by the company). The Trust in turn purchased company stock, the price of which was determined annually by a qualified stock appraiser.

This offered the company two advantages: 1) it reduced taxes on profits as a result of the deducted contribution, and 2) it provided the company capital which in our case was used to acquire the partner's holdings. To the employees it offered the advantages of 1) ownership in the company at no cost to them, 2) the powers that come with ownership: election of directors, etc., and 3) a tax-deferred benefit to be cashed in later or rolled over into a personal tax-deferred plan.

In a financial sense the ESOP did precisely what we intended it to do. However, since we installed our ESOP, one of the early ones, the rules have been modified. To assure it suits their company's goals, anyone interested in adopting an ESOP today should thoroughly research the prevailing law before doing so.

In a human relations and strategic sense, it caused a few problems.

As I've also indicated, though it solved the buyout problem, it meant the company would have to bare its soul to its employees. Everyone would vote at a stockholders' meeting on every matter that came before it. They would be privy to the company's financial statements and would participate in electing the directors. Theoretically, under our state law, they could even terminate me as their CEO if they considered me incompetent.

I found none of this troublesome, especially since I favored employee participation in making management decisions. Since I ran a fairly open company anyway, even if not quite as open as the ESOP required, the transition was hardly wrenching.

The trouble started a few years later when key employees quit, retired or were fired. Under the trust agreement the company was obligated to purchase the stock of these parties soon after their departure - unless, according to a clause of doubtful enforceability, the payout jeopardized the company's financial health.

Our sales had been falling due to a slowdown in the economy; the quarterly interest payments due the ex-partner and the bank were straining our cash flow. For good reason, our sales manager dismissed a salesman who had accumulated a substantial portion of the ESOP's shares. He demanded immediate payment. We refused under the "financial health" clause. He hired a lawyer and threatened to take us to court. Having enough problems wrestling with the effects of the recession, we hardly needed this distraction.

Borrowing against an already much diminished credit line, we paid him off. For the first time we recognized that the ESOP offered no free ride; it contained a trap or two.

But the salesman episode was only prelude to the big trouble that soon followed. Two years earlier, during the era of hostility between my ex-partner and myself, several key people left to start their own business in competition with us. There was bitterness between our companies as they raided us, wooing away some of our best people. In this instance we wished despite our dire financial straits, to purchase the stock of these ex-employees lest they (and consequently our competitor) have access to our financial statements, our plans and our latest strategies. Nowhere in the trust agreement was it mandated an employee had to sell his stock, only if he wished to do so. He must first offer it to the ESOP and if it refused, then to the company. We were again in a trap: the ex-employees refused to sell.

Their attendance at our next stockholders meeting was equivalent to having the enemy in our midst. Before the loyal assembled group, they demanded privileged information, which, contrary to the rules, I refused to provide. In every instance they also voted contrary to the rest of the employees. Their mission was clearly to agitate. But the hostility they aroused made them increasingly uncomfortable. At each quarterly meeting for the next year, they remained a festering sore. Our only weapon was to refuse to cooperate and challenge them to force us to by legal means.

Eventually they tired of the battle and decided to cash in their holdings. As much as we had tried to cover all eventualities when we installed the ESOP, we had failed to anticipate the problems that developed.

Over the next five years the company cured its debt, slowed its expansion, and accumulated cash. How would the employees react were I to put the company up for sale and refuse to sell my share to the ESOP on an installment basis? Done with risk, I wanted cash. Would they balk?

After finding a third party who valued the company at two-and-one-half-times book, provided the ESOP would also sell its share, I held my breath. At a stockholders meeting everyone saw the deal was too good to pass up - "a bird in hand" - and voted to sell. After the deal was done, I felt the relief of freedom. The truth was I had given up more autonomy than I realized. Had I another acceptable choice to buy out my partner, I would, in hindsight, have chosen it.

The Business Partnership: Marriage without Sex

Until my equal partner ceased being silent, we had an ideal relationship. He put up the seed money, contributed his prestigious name to the bank loans, and I ran the show. It was our business: his investment, my creative outlet. Though we had different reasons, our joint purpose was obviously to make the business successful. Once that was firmly assured after seven years, he concluded there was no limit to the company's growth and announced he would drop his other interests and actively participate in its management. Thus the conditions implicit in our relationship were disastrously altered.

Having had to struggle most of my life, I was cautious and far less ambitious. I refused to share his dream of empire; our purposes diverged.

When I asked what he intended to do and what function he would serve, he said he would take over sales, a position I had already promised our top salesman. I protested; he replied, in more graphic terms than I express here, that an owner's rights must take precedence over any employee's. Fearing I would lose our best salesman I used all my persuasive powers, including a substantial salary increase, to keep him from bolting. However the rift between the salesman and his owner/boss, my partner, would never close.

As our plastics materials company continued to grow at 20 to 30 percent during the next few years (as mentioned earlier, we started a satellite facility, the first of several planned, in the midwest), so did profits. Since these were high inflation years, the long-term debt incurred as we expanded was an easy burden. Our substantial growth and profits were also forgiving, covering up an accumulation of inefficiencies and bad habits.

I looked the other way as my partner regularly reported to work at 10 A.M. and left to play golf or go sailing at 3 P.M. while I put in long hours. I looked the other way as he quoted prices often based on careless calculations which resulted in losses. We were making money; why make a fuss? I could live with his looseness and his blunders so long as he respected the line that divided our labor and responsibilities.

But I couldn't look the other way when he granted a wage increase to an executive under my authority after I had already refused. Nor could I look the other way when he hired an executive whom I had earlier rejected in favor of another. After I angrily confronted him, he contritely promised to stay on his side of the line.

The big blowup only came after the oil embargo struck and the bottom line showed a major monthly loss, our first. Believing we had entered a long term recession, I wanted to reduce staff, lay off workers, and cut our substantial personal salaries by half. He, on the other hand, insisted that "my" recession was merely a temporary inventory adjustment, that the plastics industry had never experienced a reversal since its inception in World War II. Being 50/50 partners, we were deadlocked. Though I alone took a wage cut, the status quo stood in all other respects and the losses mounted.

Certainly it was a power struggle, but it was also a conflict between our life views and values. He measured success quantitatively in monetary terms and, I, qualitatively in terms of personal satisfaction. He had a mystical belief everything in life worked out for the best. But I believed that rarely would anything good happen unless I caused it. Neither one of us was right or wrong; we simply no longer tolerated our differences.

To assert my power I formulated a novel plan: I went on strike. I said nothing and disappeared, remaining incognito for three weeks and let my partner struggle alone with the chaos. It was an act akin to that of a father watching his son go to war and possibly be killed.

It worked. When I returned I found him drowning in problems in virtually every area of the business. And he was outraged I had deserted him in time of an emergency. Then he broke down and cried, begging I never abandon him again. It was a heartrending moment. Until then, he hadn't appreciated the responsibility I had assumed and he learned he wanted no part of it. He finally realized I had been putting much more into the business than he. And I understood he would never put as much into it as I.

We both knew our partnership had to come to an end. I agreed to return under certain conditions: he would respect my area of authority and I his. He would not interfere in the implementation of my plan to cut back; he would reduce his salary to that of mine; and we would take steps to sell the company to a third party. He willingly accepted, except he offered to buy me out. I had no objection. Remember, at the end of each fiscal year we drew up an agreement establishing a realistic value of the company.

Because the causes of our partnership failure would apply to any human relationship, let me sum them up as follows: 1) The purpose of our relationship had changed. 2) Work was unequally divided. 3) There ceased to be an agreement on who had what kind of power. 4) There were sharp differences in values and in viewing life. 5) And at least one party felt he was getting less than he was putting in.

[Dissatisfaction in any one of these areas is enough to end a relationship. By keeping them in mind, I was able to understand most of the relationships in the company - including customers and vendors - and see which were healthy and which were doomed to fail.]

We couldn't say one of us was more the cause than the other. We were who we were.

The divorce rate among married couples in the U.S. is 50 percent. Is there a statistic on the divorce rate among business partners? I'll take a guess: 95 percent.

CHAPTER IV

THE SUPREME TEST

Worse Than Recession

By the time the buyout was consummated, the company had lost its best key people in one devastating stroke: its top salesman, its production vice president, and its creative technical director. That wasn't all; the defectors virtually cloned our company in direct competition with us.

Perhaps they did this more for self-preservation than enmity or to better themselves. As employees, all were well compensated and had brilliant futures. But my partner and I had been locked in a war of attrition for almost two years. Like children of parents on the verge of divorce, they, and most of the employees for that matter, felt insecure. Moreover, even if the company had survived the struggle, these individuals couldn't have chosen among the remaining partners. They chose instead to combine their talents and take a chance on their own.

They possessed other qualifications that gave them an advantage over most competitors who would enter the fray. They were privy to our special production methods and quality control techniques that, until the partnership war began, had placed us on a 25 to 50 percent growth curve during the previous five years. They were also familiar with our unique manufacturing equipment which had been modified to make our process more efficient.

Not until years later did we learn they had contacted our suppliers to purchase machinery identical to ours. Nor did we know that after working hours they had secretly copied, on our copier yet, our company's customer list, our quotations (as a manufacturer of custom products we had no price lists or standard prices) and our confidential formulations - the very core of our expertise.

This was worse than having to deal with a recession. At least then every competitor is generally harmed alike. Knowing in part what information our new competitors had, we estimated we might lose 20 percent to 30 percent of our sales. Fearful of their advantage, we waited for the blows that had to come.

And indeed they did.

We first received a clue of their presence when we began losing orders on price: In case after case we were slightly underbid. After a string of disappointments, we dropped our prices, sometimes below cost to maintain our position. But we knew this would be counterproductive in the long run. We wondered where it would end.

Then our field salesmen reported customers were troubled by rumors our company was consumed with a mighty partnership struggle and was close to bankruptcy. Actually, the company was amply financed and, in fact, shortly after the defection, my partner and I settled our differences and I agreed to buy him out.

But the damage didn't end there. As soon as our competitors began expanding, they turned to raiding us of our most talented workers, and wooing away our second-string managers. The very staff people we had promoted to replace those who had left. Thus they were the most resourceful of enemies, knowing our precise strengths and how to drain us step by step. We were like a battlefield casualty slowly bleeding to death.

Morally outraged, after six months of taking blow after blow and uncertain how best to cope, we struck back.

*As CEO I personally visited every account to explain what had transpired between my partner and myself. I stated unequivocally that as majority stockholder, I would be directing the business from then on.

*To those customers and vendors who had serious doubts about our staying power, we revealed our audited balance sheet.

*After our lawyer filed for an injunction against our competitor to prohibit them from spreading false rumors about us, a judge shut them down for a month until they agreed to comply.

*I sent a notice to the trade through publications and mailings that our company had adopted an Employee Stock Ownership Plan (ESOP). Our motto became: "When you're talking to one of our employees, you're talking to the owner."

*We installed a sophisticated computer that enabled our lab to gradually reformulate our products into a more economical configuration, thus giving us a new price advantage.

Then we waited to see what effect our strategy of truth and candor would have on our seemingly precarious future. During the next year sales continued to slowly sink, but at a declining rate, finally leveling off 25 percent below the previous year. Then a remarkable series of significant events occurred.

Satisfied we were not in the dire shape rumor claimed, customers returned to us with renewed fervor. In fact, a few ensured we got their business by allowing us the opportunity to meet our competitors' prices.

Several of our best former employees who had been seduced by higher wages suddenly asked to be hired back.

They found the new competitor's benefits less generous than ours, and the cost of traveling to a more distant plant prohibitive.

Our former technical director, a stockholder in the competing company, was chagrined to learn his minority rights there were of little value. Disenchanted, he offered to return to his old job, but reluctantly we declined: A divorce is a divorce.

One of our former technicians, acquired by our new competitor with false promises of paid vacations in Greece, visited our office. Angry over the deception, he revealed the earlier theft of confidential information from our files. In a rancorous gesture, he had actually stripped their files of formulations and offered them to us. He asked us to join him in a suit against his employer. We declined. We were satisfied justice was done.

Within two years we had recovered 90 percent of the business that had been lost. Four years later, after our company had adopted a series of incentive plans, sales resumed its earlier growth curve. Ten years after the defection, we sold the company for more than two-and-one-half times its book value, providing our long-term owner/employees - those who were patient and ultimately loyal - more cash than they had ever had in their lives.

Meanwhile, our competitors remained in business (their competence was never in doubt), but after a number of years, these partners, too, bloodied themselves in their own war of attrition.

Always Take a Second Look
(A Difference with the Board of Directors)

In the 36 months it had existed, the midwest operation had never turned a profit. More recently, its losses had been increasing due to a deepening economic slowdown. I had taken the position we should shut it down, mothball it until the economy recovered, and service its market from our east coast plant which had plenty of idle capacity. At a board meeting, I had prepared an exhibit on the blackboard of a hypothetical P & L showing the sums we could save by adopting my proposal. Before our breakup, my partner had refused, arguing three years hadn't allowed the operation sufficient time to prove itself.

Not only did I consider his stand unrealistic, I saw it as rooted in pride. He couldn't bear the idea of backsliding. A policy difference between 50/50 partners leads only to stalemate. This was but one of our many disputes. After the split I expected to have my own way. This proved to be naive.

At the first board meeting after my partner's departure, the agenda called for tackling the continuing problem of the midwest plant's hemorrhaging losses.

Not wishing to exacerbate the conflict between the partners, the five-member board (of which I was chairman) had formerly remained non-committal about the facility. Now, expressing their true thoughts, the members insisted my partner was correct. They reasoned the company had spent a substantial amount getting started and had established a foothold in the midwest that could not be served as well from the east coast. Moreover, abandonment would mean losing a cadre of competent and trained workers.

Thinking all along they had been solidly behind me in the battle with my partner, I was extremely upset. Though tempted to use my power as the majority stockholder to overrule them, I knew to do so would certainly destroy their motivation to serve. I gave in under condition we would review its status in six months, a face-saving proposal to which they readily agreed.

Still, I found the constant drain the operation imposed on us hard to swallow. The board, by its action, had forced me to search for a new approach, one that would have to be more creative than simply calling it quits. Feeling the answer might lie somewhere in the P & L statement, I searched for clues. Since the midwest operation replicated the larger one in the east, utilizing identical machinery and processes, a comparison of costs between the two plants was fairly valid. What I discovered was a revelation.

On comparing both plants' variable (controllable) costs as a percentage of sales, I found the midwest plant's expenses dramatically higher: labor 25 percent more, shipping 50 percent, phone 200 percent, raw materials inventory 50 percent, and production waste 300 percent.

The figures showed in part I had diagnosed our problem as weak sales. The real problem was poor management. The midwest manager, a local man and the third in three years, had been hired for his proven managerial expertise. Always cooperative and congenial he appeared to be dedicated. His management style, however, was far less consensual than ours. And he insisted on doing things "his way" rather than "our way," which often led to conflict between him and the east coast staff.

I flew to the midwest facility. For two days and nights the manager and I reviewed the startling contrasts between the two operations' figures. We discussed in detail ways to bring costs in line. He felt confident he could not only match our performance but surpass it. Although I failed to discover precisely why his costs were higher, I departed feeling optimistic.

It was wishful thinking. After three months nothing had changed and the acrimony between him and the east coast staff had worsened. Though I loathed the idea of having to hire a fourth manager in a little over three years, and had lost confidence in my ability to find the right person, I began thinking of a replacement. What had I been doing wrong; what had I missed?

The manager's distance from headquarters was a factor; he had more autonomy than our east coast manager. He was also a local man who wasn't as familiar with the ways and culture of the eastern plant. Finally, being distant and separate, he didn't feel, and we didn't help him to feel, that we were all one company.

Wouldn't it be smart to choose a man from within, one of "our own" men, trained at the mother plant, already in tune with our culture, and a proven quantity? I approached three supervisors. None was willing to relocate regardless of a substantial wage increase and other incentives. Consequently, after dropping some qualifications and considering second echelon candidates, I chose a foreman with only a high school education, but a hard worker, imaginative in the way he performed tasks and, most important, a man who had won the respect of the men who worked for him. I offered him a substantial wage increase and a potential year-end bonus of 10 percent of the operation's pre-tax profit. He took the job.

Six months passed after my wish to close the midwest plant had been overruled. Our new man had been on the job only two months and the operation had not yet shown any significant improvement. It was time for the board to convene and to reconsider the fate of the midwest operation. This time I changed my tune - to everyone's surprise - and endorsed keeping it going. I said I had taken a second look and found I had blamed weak sales for the plant's troubles but later realized it was really due to flawed management. I yearned to give the operation a new chance to succeed. And it did - within a year.

Five years later, still under the same manager, its figures became the envy of the east's. In fact, during the next economic downturn it generated sufficient cash flow to offset the east's unprecedented losses.

Two Cultures, One Company
(The story from another angle - another lesson)

What were we doing wrong at our midwest satellite plant? During the three years of its existence we had gone through three managers. The first manager was irresponsible, the second overly ambitious and the third incapable of making wise decisions. He was also, as we later learned, on the take. Contrast this with our headquarters plant in the east where for almost 20 years we had had only three managers. The most recent one was there for seven years and his predecessor for 10. What were we doing right at the mother plant?

When we decided to open a second plant in order to better service the midwest market, it seemed we merely had to clone our existing facility to assure the new operation's success. Both plants had similar equipment, produced the same class of products by means of identical processes, and followed the same administrative procedures. Yet within months we detected differences: coming from an area of auto workers our employees were more militant than the ones in the east; they tended to be younger, more lax, less innovative. More upsetting was their seeming refusal to identify with the company - they held themselves aloof. And their absentee rate was horrible.

Whether the workers' behaviour emanated from regional tradition or the managerial styles of our various managers was a mystery. In any case, finding it intolerable we strove to develop the excellent esprit de corps prevailing at "home." We granted the same generous benefits which included employee stock ownership, and allowed them to retain the four-day week voted down in the east.

We gave them considerable autonomy as a bottom line unit, hoping this would be a spur. They even shared control over the local sales force, encouraging a crucial, close contact with customers. With rare exceptions they could set their own prices. In essence they were free to act as an independent enterprise with the advantage of having a rich parent to fall back on and to consult when in trouble. But, like children anxious to assert themselves, they insisted on taking off in fruitless directions rather than heeding the hard-learned lessons the mother plant passed on to them.

During visits, I was appalled to find them struggling with technical problems we had solved years before. Or I would discover them following policies and procedures we had long ago abandoned as counterproductive - despite the intensive headquarters training that each manager had prior to assuming control. Nevertheless, occasionally they would devise a technique or a method superior to the one in use. This occurred so infrequently the overall good effects were negligible.

Clearly, our satellite plant was, in effect, a stranger. We had given birth to an intractable child that bore no resemblance to the parent. As a consequence, we wondered whether it was worth the bother, whether we had made a mistake by getting pregnant in the first place. Since times were slow and the operation had become a drain on our resources - both financially and emotionally - we thought of shutting it down. As related in the previous section, my board of directors convinced me otherwise. Too much had been invested and the potential was too great to give up so soon.

We embarked on an exchange program, rotating employees for short stints between the two plants in the hope the correct ways of the trained people from the east would prove contagious. In effect, we were trying to superimpose one culture upon another. Initially we were encouraged. The midwest workers who spent time at headquarters were impressed and they adapted, but once back in their home environment they eventually reverted to the old pattern. And though our eastern workers exhibited a certain missionary zeal at the midwest facility, the natives reverted to their old religion soon after the eastern workers left.

I was at a loss. Nothing I had tried - new managers, centralized control, autonomy or cross-facility exposure - had worked to bring this alien child around to its parent's way of doing things. What was the magic that had made us successful at headquarters? During the years we had culled those who didn't fit in. The survivors were as one in philosophy, approach, inventiveness and style. A tacit mutual approval existed. Every move was deliberate, every procedure had a defined purpose, there was a coherence to our daily activities. We were somehow joined in a single mission that transcended profits.

Wasn't all this missing at the satellite plant? **During the weeks our midwest managers were in training, and** during their later months on the job, the headquarters staff (myself included) failed to inculcate the subtle attributes of our culture. Nevertheless it would have been futile in cases where the midwest manager and the home culture were incompatible. When I awoke to this fact, I concluded the only answer was to appoint a midwest manager from within our own distinctive culture at the home plant.

We chose a man from the shop floor who, although having no formal authority, was respected by his colleagues for his decisiveness and judgement. Furthermore he had left a leadership position with another employer to take a lesser job with us because he was more comfortable with our business approach.

The choice proved out. In the months after his installation, the midwest operation slowly transformed itself into a miniature clone of the mother plant and moved into the black. The two cultures now spoke a common language and had become one. For the first time the plants belonged to each other. Not surprisingly, years later under "our" man's capable aegis the midwest plant surpassed the parent.

Change Your Corporate Culture - And Win
A Letter to the Editor of
The Wall Street Journal

As a former employee of both large and small companies for 16 years and later as CEO of a closely held manufacturing enterprise for 20 years, I am impelled to take issue with Peter Drucker's March 28th, 1992 article in *The*

Wall Street Journal, "Don't Change Corporate Culture - Use It".

I have no argument with Mr. Drucker's thesis that "There is a --- need to change deeply ingrained habits in a good many organizations," and the contemporary needs of business, "require --- changes in behavior." But we part company when he states categorically that "changing behavior works only if it can be based on the existing culture."

Mr. Drucker may well be correct when he attributes culture to the failures of India and China to adapt to economic reforms. However, one can also point to other cultures where radical change has been successful. Take the the transformation of Nazi Germany from dictatorship to post-war democracy. If the ancient ways of Chinese culture are so fundamental and recalcitrant, how do we explain its adaptation to Communism on one hand, and on the other the success of modern capitalism among the mainland Chinese on Taiwan? Or pockets of thriving free enterprise in Communist China? Cultures do evolve and accept modification as needs change - leading either to their enrichment or destruction.

I disagree with Mr. Drucker's counsel that, "If you have to change habits, don't change culture." This smacks of the behaviorists' view that we can change our ways without knowing their origin or understanding their historic (and currently obsolete) role. Such behavior changes are superficial. To assure a change is solidly a part of ourselves, we must also change our attitude, our way of thinking, perhaps even our values, our beliefs and customs. In short, a part of our culture.

But which level of culture does Mr. Drucker suggest we ignore? Does he mean, when referring to other national cultures, our Western American culture? Or does he recommend we ignore the various sub-cultures: the company's, the region's, the ethnic group's, the family's. Assuming the larger culture is consistent with a company's goals (and often this is in doubt), can the same be said for it's inherent micro-culture?

One company I worked for was notable for the fear its CEO's cruel arbitrariness aroused in its employees. Another succeeded in generating distrust and suspicion among its employees because its CEO rarely kept a promise. Another had universally angry employees who went on strike against a stingy, adversarial management every other year. And another made its employees feel important and secure under a caring and respecting management.

These are a few of the micro-cultures I encountered in the multitude of jobs I held from factory worker to assistant to the CEO. In every instance, including the largest corporation and the smallest private firm of just a few employees, the company was a hierarchical dictatorship. Usually the cultural ethos was antipathetic to the company's stated goals. It rarely motivated the employees, and generally failed to promote efficiency, thus minimizing the firm's potential for profits.

In most cases it would have been futile to take Mr. Drucker's advice to expect "results --- not by doing something different but by systematically doing something everyone had known all along should be done, had in policy manuals and had been preaching ---." Quite the contrary. The employees in those companies were doing precisely what they were told to do, what the "book" said to do, but not what they, if consulted, would prefer to do in the interest of the company.

Ironically, within our democratic tradition, our business sub-culture is resoundingly anti-democratic. How big a leap would it be for a business to change from a culture in which managers give commands, to one in which employees participate in matters concerning their specific jobs or even beyond? We all acknowledge ruling by consent of the governed leads to greater human happiness. And we agree a free and contented people is generally more creative and productive - to which our country gives ample testimony. To convert a business from dictatorship to democracy (for the purpose of improving the bottom line) involves far more than simply changing behavior, or following a policy manual as Mr. Drucker would have us do. Such a conversion, however, is not beyond us as Americans to appreciate and admire.

I agree with Mr. Drucker when he writes: "--- changing habits and behavior requires changing recognitions and rewards." During my CEO years, I found "recognitions and rewards" were powerful motivating factors, endemic not only to our culture but also to our human need for approval. But they could also lead to excessive competitiveness, the exploitation of others, overweening ambition and ultimate inefficiencies. In other words, reward for individualistic behavior would often negate team effort which is so essential to the smooth running of an enterprise. Unfortunately, the very nature of an organization requires sacrificing to some extent an individual's special interests. More than once for the sake of peace we had to fire competent, superior individuals for whom recognition and reward weren't enough.

Team reward proved to be something else. Here cooperation is encouraged rather than the competitiveness engendered by individual reward. Here the superior person is expected to contribute that superiority in both monetary and recognition terms. Of course, it's for a cause beyond himself or herself. It's for the team, and ultimately the company. It works. We did it. Yet the team principle runs counter to our deeply rooted individualistic behavior. Though our employees undertook a radical cultural adjustment to become team oriented, they suddenly seemed more relaxed, more cooperative, more dedicated and more secure on the job after they participated in a team incentive system.

And Mr. Drucker, this was all new. We had already used up old procedures that no longer worked by the time we realized our company had not only to change its ways, but also its culturally based assumptions.

Certainly to make changes consistent with our culture is far easier as Mr. Drucker urges. Nor are changes always necessary. Although the American automotive industry would rather lobby our government to restrict imports, the industry need not undergo a cultural change to make better cars. Nor does it require a cultural change to revise the American corporate habit of granting outlandish monetary rewards to top executives for mediocre performance. Our culture has a penchant for making things "good enough" rather than striving to make them "perfect," an attitude the Japanese were known to have before World War II. They changed and their culture remained intact. But it may take a change in our culture to overcome the adversarial tendencies of American business. There's a reluctance to cooperate with those on whom a business depends.

In fact, I suggest American business must change some of the general aspects of its micro-culture, otherwise it may fall behind businesses within cultures, both local and national that recognize and meet the need for excellence in today's increasingly competitive global economy. This may require a wrenching revision of our own national culture by leaders who refuse to coddle mediocrity and dare to question our present failing values.

Business: The Perpetual War

When I started in industry, my boss used to say: "I'm all for the competitive system, except the part I'm in." Decades later, in 1977, as CEO of my own intensely competitive plastics coloring materials business, I felt the same way. Indeed you would have dubbed me the Henry Higgins ("My Fair Lady") of the business world if you heard me complain, "Why can't a customer be more like a friend?"

A shocking thing happened to our company. Our biggest customer, one of America's largest plastics consumers, whose purchases constituted one third of our sales, seemed to be abandoning us for no reason. For the first five years of our relationship we were their sole supplier because no competitor could match either our quality or our service. Not that our customer hadn't tried time and time again to find additional sources. When eventually they did, we understood. After all, we too were proponents of multiple sourcing wherever possible.

In fact, we felt an unanticipated sense of relief when their orders leveled off. As that customer's purchases occupied a larger portion of our total sales, we grew increasingly uncomfortable. It had already become necessary to install extra production machinery (and increase long-term debt) just to maintain the high grade service they expected. How do you tell a customer - or yourself - you don't want more business?

When we noticed a gradual, yet steady, drop in their purchases we became alarmed. After asking the reason for the decline, our salesman for the account reported it was only temporary - their product sales were off. Really? Historically, the customer, a global manufacturer of a uniquely recession-proof line of quality plastic housewares, had experienced steady sales growth through both good times and bad - and times were still good.

The decline continued for most of the year until the additional machinery we had dedicated to serving their demands stood idle on our plant floor. Despite pressuring our sales staff to drum up sales elsewhere, we were unable to compensate for the loss of business fast enough. It was time to confront the king and find out what was truly going on in Denmark - presumably something rotten.

And it was indeed rotten from our perspective. The customer confessed to gradually installing an in-house operation to manufacture the products we had been supplying. The only orders we were receiving were for items whose manufacture they had not yet mastered.

Our initial reactions were anger and hurt. Is this treatment we should expect after a decade-long relationship? We had given this customer our best. We had worked holidays and Sundays at double-time to meet their frequent emergencies, produced a product that met specifications far stricter than any required by the rest of the trade. Is this proper consideration from a customer whose welfare we had placed ahead of the more than 300 other accounts in our roster?

The silence of our excess equipment troubled us. Not knowing how committed the customer was to its course, we submitted a proposal we expected would at least give them pause. The customer admitted having periodic difficulty matching our quality. Our own employees, some of whom had relatives employed by the company, said it was experiencing unprecedented downtime on its production lines. Our proposal: After revealing our costs, we would arrive at a mutually agreed on price that would allow us a reasonable profit.

We were offering drastic price reductions since we had been selling from strength and had commanded comfortable margins. It was doubtful the customer could ever expect to match our low costs. Typical of most large corporations, its operation was loaded with overhead far exceeding ours. We also suggested it was difficult to acquire our kind of expertise. "We can hire all the experts we need," was the reply. We were turned down categorically. In a few months orders ceased.

Three years later our sources told us the (former) customer still had problems duplicating our quality. In order to minimize downtime on its production lines, it had to compromise and accept sub-standard in-house material it would have rejected from us. To attain the quality we had achieved had taken five years, and further improvement was continuing. The customer had obviously underestimated the length of the learning curve.

It had made a grave blunder. If reducing costs was the primary goal, it could have had that immediately. Instead, the start-up, including an over-investment in people and ultra-sophisticated equipment, severely increased costs. (Big companies rarely keep it simple, preferring to go all out.) More likely, it wished to control the source of its coloring supplies. Had it tested us it might have succeeded in buying us out. Or if not all, possibly a piece of us. Everything then would have been in place. They would have a stable full of customers to keep production going around the clock, further reducing unit costs.

Why must business relationships be so adversarial in our country? Initially denying its intentions, our customer deceived us and gave us no warning. Had we known earlier we would have been able to take precautions, certainly not add machinery. And when we were willing to bare our secrets, we were shut off. A brutality underlies all business relationships, not only between competitors but also between management and worker, customer and supplier, the company and the bank.

The Japanese have devised a support system, the keiretsu. It consists of a group of interlocking companies, often including a bank, as a competitive entity that works effectively towards eliminating duplication and waste generated by inefficient competition among fellow members. Our approach to the customer had been a feeble step toward that end.

As a mature company we probably would have welcomed joining a keiretsu if they existed here. On the other hand, if such groups were pervasive, how would we have started, who would have helped finance us, and how would we have broken into an established, closed system? Perhaps we need both systems operating in tandem. Still, given the system we've got, I ask: Why can't a customer, an employee, a supplier, and a banker be more like a company's friend?

Who Says the Big Boys Are Smarter?

As CEO of a small company, I looked up to the managements of big corporations as examples of how to do things properly. Given their enormous size, I felt safe in assuming the giants got that way by means of the skill, if not the genius, of their top managements. Of course, many large corporations do fail - Pan Am, Bank of New England and Chrysler are examples. But it doesn't happen often. In my small company, management's every mistake was glaring and often had immediate consequences. Corporate managers are typically shielded from the effects of their blunders which often remain undiscovered for months, years, or possibly forever. Size is truly forgiving. But the proof my assumption wasn't correct became evident as I witnessed the inefficiency and decline of so many of the giants during hard times. Several years ago I explored with IBM the purchase of a then-innovative computer system for our laboratory - a package of hardware and software. So arrogant were IBM's representatives that we, the customer, felt like supplicants seeking a king's favor. Worse, we had to consult one layer after another of experts to get answers. Some never materialized. As a result, we gave up in disgust and delayed computerizing our lab until we found a dedicated smaller company. After this experience I had heard similar stories about IBM from other companies.

What baffled me at the time was IBM's incredible success. After the way we were treated, their expertise aside, how could they remain in business, let alone continue to grow? But grow they did until the recession of '90-92. It has taken decades for the error of their ways to surface under pressure of competition. At last they are reorganizing into smaller, product and service-specific entities which are more accountable, more efficient and humanly manageable. It's an organizational approach IBM should have followed decades ago.

Which brings me to a more recent event that shows that dealing with a big boy doesn't necessarily mean dealing with a smart one. I wrote the following letter to the chairman and CEO of a global high-tech company whose sales in 1991 approached $2.7 billion.

"Dear Mr. Chairman, As a holder of 1,900 shares of XYZ stock, most of which was purchased when it was in the $40 plus range (it's now around $9), I am intensely interested in XYZ's present and future state. I must confess to a frequently nagging question: should I just take my lumps, sell and invest in a stock with more potential or should I hang in, as I have already done for so long, on the gamble that XYZ has seen the light.

"Apparently XYZ has lacked the wisdom to realize that the only way to stay ahead of its competitors and remain more than marginally profitable in a swiftly changing field is by developing and marketing more advanced products than the competitors - not following the narrow, short term and self-defeating course of producing more goods in an increasingly glutted market. In other words, why be a great big commodity company making less money with enormous effort when you can be a great smaller advanced company making more money with less effort?

"Often over the years when I've read XYZ's annual report, how frustrated I've felt over the lack of mention of any new products being launched. And this week how frustrated I continued to be when I perused the company's expensive presentation of its year-end report (showing a loss). This in no way enhances the company's profitability which is, after all, what every stockholder wishes to see as a recent survey of stockholders who deplored the excesses of their companies has indicated in *The Wall Street Journal*. A simple presentation may not save much, but how powerfully symbolic it is.

"By the way, enclosed is an article on how the undersigned once coped with a recession, although I was not faced with your problem of being in a swiftly moving industry. I realize you have recently re-assumed the top operating job, and I trust you do so fully aware of the error of XYZ's former ways. Maybe I ought to wait, give you a chance, before I decide whether to sell or not. What are my chances of winning?"

In reply, I had hoped to hear that: steps were being taken to stanch the losses, a new strategy was in effect to guarantee future growth, R & D was working hard to place the company in the forefront of the industry once again, and he, as CEO would do everything within his power to make my investment pay off. Perhaps some words of encouragement and even a little PR.

Instead I received, along with my returned letter, the following hand-written note:

"Mr. Aaron ----

"1. I never offer advice on trading any securities, including XYZ's.

"2. I don't think the WSJ article on annual reports is pertinent. Our annual report is mainly a marketing tool, followed by usage with vendors, new employees, and existing employees. If it were done strictly for shareholders, our approach would be quite different.

"3. We're working hard during some pretty tough times."

After reading the note, I handed it and my letter to my non-business oriented wife for comment. "Let's sell," was all she said.

Here was a CEO who appeared tactless, rigid, defensive and without any sensitivity to human relationships - especially with respect to stockholders. Could this be one of the major problems of his troubled company? During an upward blip I sold half the stock. A new generation of his industry's products will be coming to market in the near future. I'll hold the other half until I see whether the company meets the challenge.

(A note just prior to publication: The company has since shown an improved quarter and the stock rose again. I then sold my remaining shares. I still had no confidence in its CEO.)

The Banker: Friend and Adversary

Business wasn't good enough to generate the cash flow I needed to meet the first of three principal (plus interest) payments due my ex-partner. Our agreement also stipulated that if I defaulted (and didn't pay within 60 days) he would take over the company.

As a result of the buyout, all the company's assets - inventory, equipment and receivables - were pledged to the bank. Four years earlier, when I signed the agreement, I believed I would have sufficient time to restore the company to health before the first principal payment came due. I couldn't have known then that interest rates would skyrocket, the economy would remain stagnant and certain key people would defect to form a competitive business.

For months, denying my days as CEO would soon be over, I put on a front that all was well. Then came a warning. An anxiety attack led me to seek counseling and eventually find the courage to face a fearful reality.

The bank had done nothing, but I knew after reviewing the statement of the then current quarter, someone would soon call. In anticipation, I met with the loan officer with whom I had a candid business relationship for more than 10 years. Though I took particular pride in not revealing panic, I couldn't hide my sense of hopelessness. Our meeting, I told him, was simply to inform the bank of my predicament.

He calmly proposed we remain optimistic and explore all possibilities, starting with a statement of my net worth. He would find nothing there, I insisted. My home was heavily mortgaged, there was a loan outstanding on my wife's car and, of course, I had personally signed the company's note to the bank.

Moving down the list of my personal assets, the loan officer stopped at "Factory Building." What was this? Nothing worthwhile, I said. I owned it outright. I bought my partner's share during the breakup. But it carried a big mortgage. How old was the mortgage? Ten years. Hadn't the building appreciated in value? After all, it was in an industrial park next to a superhighway interchange, a prime location. He would have it appraised.

Was I on the brink of being reprieved?

The next day the loan officer called, genuinely excited. The appraisal figure was given at four times the building's original value. The bank, therefore, would take a 15-year mortgage sufficient to cover the entire note. By spreading payments over 15 years rather than three years, I could enhance cash flow. But why not offer my ex-partner a lump sum payment for less?

That hadn't occurred to me. But with funds available, I could be daring. I proposed a settlement 50 percent less than the amount originally negotiated. He was outraged.

I reminded him the company had been paying only 8 percent interest on the note, while he could earn 12 percent or more (the prevailing rate) in Treasuries or CD's. Furthermore, in view of the shaky economy, the company's future ability to pay wasn't assured. If we were to continue our slide, I said, I might do some drastic stripping. There was no telling then how much the value of our assets would decline by the time, and in case, he took over. A week later, he returned with a compromise to which I agreed. At last, I was free of the note and its haunting promise of disaster.

I owed this remarkable outcome to the banker. He had loyally applied himself and took visible satisfaction in finding a solution. Until then I considered him as simply a source of funds. Now I understood the creative role he could play.

It was difficult two years later when I felt compelled to change banks. Interest rates had risen to 18 percent (eventually they reached 21 percent); and it seemed the company existed solely for the benefit of the bank. Despite appeals, and warnings that I would be forced to seek relief elsewhere, I failed to secure any concession from the friendly loan officer.

After months of sounding out the big city banks, I found a secure small bank of a size adequate for our needs. So favorable were its terms (no minimum checking account balance, no insurance on my life, no pledge of receivables, a below-prime interest rate) that when I presented them to our large regional bank to match, they were incredulous.

Two years later, a new loan officer from our old bank visited my office. The bank was ready to meet the competition. Was I interested? I wouldn't simply dump the sort of mutually respectful relationship that had developed with the new bank.

Besides, the new loan officer was a stranger. Perhaps had the old loan officer called on me I might have split the business. But he had moved "upstairs" out of sight.

The CEO as Superman

One hot Monday in August as I was driving on the superhighway, I began having difficulty breathing and felt a tightness in my chest. The manager of our midwest plant and his wife, and a midwest salesman were with me. We planned to stop for lunch on the way to the airport before they caught a flight to Cleveland.

We were returning from a company paid weekend at a resort where our entire administrative, sales and production staffs and their spouses gathered to review our company's fortunes and plan future strategy. Business wasn't bad but it could have been better.

Sipping only water and unable to eat, the "attacks" continued. When my guests expressed concern, I put them off, muttering it was only indigestion. But by the time we returned to the car, I suspected something worse. I drove to a hospital. I insisted they drop me off, continue on their way and leave my car at the airport.

I told the nurse I thought I was having a heart attack. She led me into a small ward, called the doctor and hooked me up to a monitor. The doctor arrived, felt my pulse, listened to my heart and watched the monitor. Then he announced I had an anxiety attack, not a heart attack.

He asked whether I had been under stress. My reply: Certainly not; things couldn't be better; everything was under control. He suggested I see my personal doctor. Meanwhile, noting my pulse was still running fast, the nurse invited me to lay back in the bed and relax for a while before departing.

Closing my eyes, I let my mind wander for the next half hour. I realized until then I had known no peace and had no time for myself. At work I was responsible for almost 100 employees; after work I was responsible for a wife, three kids and a big mortgage.

My doctor, remarking that stress apparently agreed with me, found me physically fit, but urged me to get to the bottom of what happened. See a psychiatrist, he said.

As with most entrepreneurs, the very idea that I couldn't handle a crisis was an insult to my ego. ME need help? Still, this anxiety business was something else; it was sneaky, and had come from inside, the place I had ignored. I suppose, in my own way, I thought I had mastered the world. Everybody around me seemed to think so too. Still I made an appointment to see the man my doctor recommended.

I thought the first few sessions were a waste of time and I told the therapist so. My family life was OK, business was good, and I had competent people working for me. This anxiety thing was a low-down trick that shouldn't have happened.

But it did happen, the doctor importuned, and it didn't happen without cause. He presented it as a challenge.

Gradually a shape began to emerge from amidst the talk and the denials. I spoke casually about buying out my partner.

The therapist probed.

The buyout consisted of a seven-year note stipulating that only interest would be payable during the first four years, but in the fifth year the first principal installment plus interest would be due. I confessed I had perhaps paid too high a price, but it was worth it. I had no regrets. After all, I wasn't about to start all over again in my 50s.

I thought I had been clever. The note was structured to provide me four years of debt relief, which I assumed was sufficient time to reorganize and restore the company to health. But I was mistaken: the economy and the bank's demands for high interest rates, hadn't cooperated. The company's progress fell short of my projections. Cash flow was insufficient. I was certain not to meet the payment due in two months.

But no one - not my employees, my wife, the customers or the suppliers - must know. I put on a smiling, confident front.

No wonder you had an anxiety attack, concluded the psychiatrist. Who wouldn't, given the circumstances? It was clear I was suffering not from a neurosis, but from too strong a dose of reality.

That was not all.

I knew I feared most what I denied was sure to happen.

A condition of the note stated that if I defaulted and didn't cure it within 60 days, I must forfeit the company in its entirety to my ex-partner. This condition had been essential in order that he would sign.

The truth was out in the open and I fell into a depression. The therapist, confessing a lack of business expertise, asked whether I had gone to the bank. How could I? Virtually the company's total collateral was pledged. It was no use.

But with nothing to lose, I called the bank's loan officer and leveled with him. The bank saved me, and my self-confidence was restored. I've had no more anxiety attacks. After that I shared the company's problems with everybody concerned. After all, I'm no superman.

Debunking Conventional Wisdom

Like parents raising a child, most people in business learn on the job. Even those of us who have attended business schools are inadequately equipped. Such facilities provide only the tools, not the essential judgement. And judgement can't be taught. Tempered by actual experience, it is an inherent quality. Only by doing, only by enduring the experience, are we truly tested as we unlearn all the notions about business that comprise conventional wisdom.

In our small company it was our willingness to cast aside those notions, to acknowledge deeper truths, that led to our survival and our continued success. What follows is a comparison of our assumptions and reality.

*By offering a superior product, superior service and a competitive price, a company is bound to succeed.

Not so. Not until we called on the trade long enough and frequently enough to establish relationships did we begin to make it. The real advantages that we offered were less important in contributing to our success than the human connections we cultivated.

*Honesty pays.

Not necessarily. Over the years we failed to sell certain major accounts because our competitors indulged in payola. We could have secured some of the business were we willing to compete on the same basis. We weren't. Morality is not a factor in determining a company's success. Honesty relieves the conscience and elevates the pride of its employees. Honest companies often have to sacrifice gain, but they are happier for it.

*Unions are good for employees, bad for companies.

Not all companies. We had no union, but our nearest competitor did. Their union struck almost every year, usually at the peak of the production season. That was good for our company. The union failed several times to organize our shop. Why? Our benefit package was superior to that offered by the union - we were an employee-owned, open company. And though our wages were slightly less than our competitors', our employees' annual take-home pay was far larger due to the absence of layoffs (as a result of job versatility, typically prohibited by unions) and strikes.

*CEO's thrive on risk.

Not this CEO. Every risk I took was calculated. I made sure we could survive a worst-case eventuality. My calculations only failed where I misjudged how bad a worst case could be - such as the loss of a major customer, an oil embargo, or an unprecedented 21 percent interest rate. Indeed, I strove to minimize risk in every policy decision I made. I didn't consider going into business much of a risk, yet it was the biggest risk of all.

*Recessions are bad for a business.

"A" is the key word. Recessions are bad for business, but not for a business. Recessions forced us to realistically examine how to survive. Indeed, they compelled our entire organization to apply its ingenuity and imagination to coping with the crisis. We adopted innovative management methods: more openness, incentive systems, the elimination of layoffs, ways of conserving materials and energy.

We learned, for instance, that internal cost cutting was more productive than struggling to increase sales in a contracting market. We learned it was wiser to take action where we had control, rather than try to contend with areas where we had minimal control. Recessions taught us new ways to manage and lessons we would never have learned had they not occurred. By ridding ourselves of past excesses, we became healthier.

*Competition eliminates poorly managed companies.

The staying power of weak companies often defies free enterprise principles. On the brink of failure, they hang on, refusing to die. Meanwhile they do considerable damage to their industry by compelling competitors to replicate their self-destructive policies in order to compete. As more suppliers come upon the scene, few, if any, do well. The industry reaches a stage of saturation, its participants dragging on year after year in a war of attrition. Not all failing companies fail. They don't even fade away. We despised them. Give us a successful competitor anytime.

*Employees distrust management.

Implicit in this statement is employee culpability - which doesn't square with reality. Prime Minister Miazawa of Japan was incorrect in condemning the American worker for being lazy. American dictatorial management is at fault. It forgets that business is a human endeavor for humans.

Employees are conditioned not to trust because management, not trusting them, is secretive and places profits ahead of the employees' welfare. Trust must be mutual. One side has to take the initiative of trusting the other. Only after we listened, invited our employees to participate in decisions affecting them, opened up our closely held company, revealed our figures and proved we were sincere in sharing, did the employees trust management and say what they truly thought. We, management and workers alike, were like birds freed from our cages.

*Administrative procedures and good record keeping are essential to a smooth running operation.

Except when they become an end in themselves. When a competitor's vice-president joined us, he was startled to learn how little paperwork we had and how brief and direct were our procedures compared with those of his former, long-established employer. Once forms and procedures are entrenched, they tend to become a way of life even after they are obviously obsolete.

*Just as management seeks first to maximize profits, employees seek first to maximize income.

Not true. Management tries most to minimize risk. Employees try to do the same by striving for security. Our company was happiest and most efficient after we eliminated layoffs. Our total employment roster consisted of a corps of long-term employees - none of whom had less than five years seniority. Create a structure of guaranteed security and most other issues will lend themselves to a ready resolution.

*The free enterprise system is just, fair and efficient.

Hardly. The income spread between most CEO's and their workers is outrageous. We have more super-rich than ever. More people receive outlandish compensation for activities (the law, accounting and financial trading) that contribute little or nothing to production and creativity. The system wastes an enormous amount of talent. Our accountant rejoiced every time Congress complicated the tax laws. And our lawyer was strikingly imaginative in manufacturing causes for adversarial action where, in our view, none existed.

It is also a system of success of the fittest. Because life is mindless, we strive to make it somewhat just. A business leader also has a choice under our system to be just or unjust. That's the wonder and often the tragedy of it.

CHAPTER V

MANAGING THROUGH RECESSION

Opening the Company

In 1981, when the economic downturn hit, we tried the logical thing: counter it with an austerity plan. Such an attempt, however, is more easily wished for than achieved. I called a company-wide meeting to inform our employees there would be no more overtime, no more quarterly bonuses, and no purchases of new machinery. Wage increases would be delayed or, if conditions worsened, eliminated. While I expected no one to be pleased, I hoped for understanding. Instead I got suspicion, resentment and innuendo.

It was the traditional American labor versus management syndrome. When I mentioned that I, too, was sacrificing by taking a wage cut, the hearsay was: yeah, from an outrageous $200,000 to $199,000. After explaining the company's most recent quarter ended in a loss, I heard snickers of doubt.

If, despite what I would say, my people didn't believe bad things were happening to the company, one alternative would be to show them. This, I learned, required an act of courage. And I was a reluctant hero. Possessive of my business, having built it through personal sacrifice and risk - from a money losing operation into a prosperous credit-worthy enterprise - I found sharing its innermost secrets anathema, akin to revealing one's sex life.

Our accountant and all my business friends were appalled at the concept, saying it was bizarre and highly dangerous. One business acquaintance warned that under such circumstances I'd have to give up my Mercedes, sail boat and country club membership. But the company didn't own a boat or belong to a country club, and I drove only a company Cressida. Anyway, were the contrary true, in hard times the trappings should be dispensable.

Wouldn't the benefits outweigh the risk? If I shared the bottom line, and the details of our expenses, wouldn't I also be sharing the burden of having to take action? The firm would change from a typically American autocratic enterprise into a uniquely democratic one. As in any democracy, openness elicits responsibility. Was I in for a few surprises!

At the end of the quarter we shut down the plant for an hour and held an all-employee meeting in the cafeteria. There on a blackboard was displayed a replica of the profit-and-loss statement. Based on questions such as "What is meant by gross profit?" and "What is the difference between fixed and variable expenses?" our executives realized that showing wasn't enough. We'd have to educate our people. It was our first surprise, symptomatic of our innocence.

After volunteering to do the job, one of our managers held daily sessions teaching small groups of employees how to interpret a P & L statement. I also appointed him to present the statement at each company-wide quarterly meeting. It was, in a sense, a continuation of his enjoyable instructive role.

From that first session on I rather relished that I was no longer a lone worrier. Now my employees could worry along with me. They would learn as insiders that being in business isn't the "picnic" they thought it was from outside. And they would have no choice but to believe what they see. Right?

Just as I began to think we had succeeded in allaying all suspicions of management's motives, I was stunned with the accusation that we kept two sets of books and the one we showed had ulterior motives. I could only marvel at the deep-seated distrust between worker and management. Knowing that my assurances would count for little, I invited the company's outside accountant (and auditor) to attend the next session to explain his role, and to validate the genuineness of the figures.

As the employees became more sophisticated the liveliness of the sessions increased. More intelligent questions were asked. My original concept that openness would promote understanding, trust and cooperation proved to be too limited. In fact, the benefits far exceeded those precious but prosaic, expectations. Another surprise.

Take, for example, a simple expense item of $4,000 that appeared on the quarterly P&L: the workers' rented uniforms. They were shocked to see the figure. They had no idea that what they wore and tossed into the laundry every day was so costly. They came forward, as one, with the remarkably simple suggestion that the company purchase the uniforms and invest in a commercial washing machine and dryer. They could then wash their own uniforms at the end of each working day before going home. After an analysis, we estimated the savings at $12,000 a year - an office worker's annual wage.

And their bottom-line thinking didn't end there. When it was learned that we spent several thousand dollars each year on a Christmas party, the employees asked that we do without one. Instead, they suggested that the accumulated earnings of our vending machines be set aside and raffled off during the holidays (a possibly illegal practice to which we all agreed).

While everyone was invited to comment on policy decisions, each employee had a direct responsibility in making the final one affecting him or her. Our janitor, knowing why we had to cut our advertising budget, for example, chose the broom he, not we, preferred to buy.

Of course, nothing goes smoothly for long in human affairs. Some individuals, unable to see beyond their own narrow interest or to identify with a larger entity, refused to sacrifice for the good of the organization no matter what the reality. Most disappointing, some of those people were in the upper echelon. Uncomfortable with our open style - or choosing to ignore it - they obviously would be better off in a traditional closed company where they would be told nothing, their responsibility would be restricted, and where they would be free only to suspect everything. That's where I suggested they go.

The Open Company - How Open?

As soon as we became an ESOP company, it was mandatory under the law that I, the CEO and owner of 80 percent of the stock, reveal our financials to the employee stockholders. Such revelations are routine in publicly owned corporations, but to me it was downright frightening - equivalent to baring my most personal secrets.

Suddenly the employees, having knowledge of every expense item, could ask questions about how and where money was spent. Knowing our bottom line when it's bad might make them feel insecure. When it's good, they might ask for wage increases or additional benefits. They could question my perks, object to my Mercedes, express outrage at my salary. The scene could be one embarrassing confrontation after another.

Yet, I believed, as a deeply held principle, employee participation in management can benefit both the company and the employees. I believed a democratic approach would ultimately promote innovation, a cooperative spirit, and would motivate the employees to perform at their peak. This was not happening under the traditional dictatorial management regimen I was practicing.

How could I square my need to manage and be in control with the employees' need to know and having a role in policy making? Intuitively I knew I had to strike a balance, but didn't know where or how. The real question was how much democracy could the business tolerate without becoming inefficient?

A democracy's survival depends on consensus. The survival of a business depends on profit. In a democracy the participants pay. In a business the participants are paid. In a democracy, consensus is voluntary. In a traditional business, consensus is bought. (Those who disagree with management don't last long.) The comparison between running a business and a democracy is barely valid. This I had to learn incident by incident until the dawn broke.

I learned that a democratically managed business requires a strong executive. With so many employees expressing themselves and so many opinions in play and so much "confidential" information available, decisiveness was absolutely necessary. Since my employees could dismiss me for incompetence (minority rights) or for not representing the interests of "their" company with which they now identified, I knew my mission had been enlarged far beyond my personal goals. Implicit in my staying power was their faith in me. In a sense, though I owned a controlling interest, I would be president by consent. My job was clear: make the company prosper in an atmosphere of mutual respect and good will.

Sometimes I withheld information if it wasn't asked for by the parties affected. In other instances I refused to provide information to avoid resentment or misunderstanding. Therefore, my style was not purely democratic, nor did it pretend to be. Still, for the most part we were an open company.

For instance: the team incentive for each production line was based on the increase in hourly output over the historical average. We could easily translate this into dollars saved to be shared with the team. How much of the savings should be shared? Obviously the answer was enough to motivate each employee. That was one third to the employee, two thirds to the company. (More on this later.) The team members, content with their monthly incentive bonus, never even asked how the gain was split. Since they too were shareholders and the two thirds portion went directly to the bottom line, they gained in that sense as well.

Why didn't we reveal the split? We suspected if we had, the team would ask for a larger share, maybe 50-50, or the opposite of what we gave. Since management devised the incentive plan, and voluntarily offered it as a way of increasing employees' earnings in return for increased effort, we felt justified in not revealing the split. The wage paid each employee was the result of an implicit bargain. In our case, the wage was generous enough so that our turnover, the true test, was negligible.

I also refused to reveal salary information. Though most hourly employees seemed to know what each was earning, none of the management staff was privy to that kind of information about themselves. Only the bookkeeper and the office manager knew what I was paid. In the quarterly P & L, which everyone in the company was free to scrutinize, wages and salaries were lumped together as an expense under various departments.

No one complained. Only the bottom line mattered, and when it was bad an explanation was sufficient to put everyone at ease. (When it was bad, I was first to take a pay cut.) In other words, they had faith that the company's welfare was in competent hands; it wasn't being exploited on behalf of myself or the staff. Indeed, when the company sold my Mercedes and bought me a Toyota, the employees objected, saying such a modest vehicle ill fitted a leader of their company. (Eventually I traded it for an Audi Turbo - which was barely acceptable to them.)

The top executive who strives to be open must not allow himself to be intimidated by the democratic form; he must not follow the political model too literally. This may have already happened in some Japanese companies. Employee participation in a company works, but only to a point. Where to draw the line between openness and efficiency depends on the particular CEO's comfort zone. But in every instance he must be the boss, he must have the final say, or else he's done for and his company will soon follow.

During Recession, Manage Defensively

Why didn't I, as CEO, anticipate the recession in order to take the proper defensive steps? Wasn't that part of my job? Wasn't I warned in advance that bad times were coming? Yes and no. Until the recession became obvious the economists' predictions were divided. Isn't that a valid excuse?

No. (Most CEO's are hard on themselves.) Once the recession struck I learned which prognosticators were correct and noted the accuracy of their predictions over the following years. Eventually, as it became clear that one in particular was correct more often, I bet on him. When the next recession, a mild one, snuck up on us, we were ready.

A further answer to the first question - why the mess? - lies in the answer to the second - what's the remedy? Though we had been drawing P & L's every month, they revealed little that was meaningful except for the bottom line. Only after we had points of reference - the figures of a comparable month with which to compare each expense item as a percent of sales - could we evaluate whether something was truly good or bad.

The "we" is not editorial. Until that crisis, I had always assumed the burden of rescuing us single-handedly. But this time I felt overwhelmed, bereft of solutions. Suddenly, it only made sense that those responsible (the VPs, managers, and supervisors) for losses (and, of course, profits) should know what they were, determine their origin and participate as a team in devising remedial procedures. This was especially true for specific profit centers in which a manager and his lieutenants were directly involved.

However, we quickly realized that the monthly P & L statement (and more so the quarterly and the annual), with its breakdown into various departmental subdivisions, often reported situations too remote for timely and effective corrective action. It would be useful if we knew how much money we had made (or lost) each day. And how much better if we could precisely identify which orders were the losers. The solution: add up the various costs (overhead applied to production-time consumed, material, labor, energy and shipping) that went into completing a particular order and compare that with what we charged the customer.

By compiling separate profit and loss figures for orders produced during the preceding 24 hours, we could review by 10 A.M. each day the P & L for the prior day. In fact, as the cumulative daily figures mounted, we knew exactly which day of the month we broke even (if we were so lucky). As a result, the bottom line on the monthly P & L which arrived several days after month's-end was never a surprise. And by the time our quarterly statement arrived the news was already ancient history. As for our annual P & L statement, this was done principally for the benefit of the bank and the IRS.

Just as our lack of information was the cause of not being able to anticipate the recession, it also caused our blindness in coping with it. Though at first we may have blamed declining sales for our predicament, we soon learned that we should have blamed our failure to pinpoint troubles and their first causes on a micro level. Either we weren't reacting correctly to the crisis or, when we did react, we were too late.

We had established a policy of cutting costs as sales declined. That was consistent with the premise that every dollar saved goes directly to the bottom line versus only part of a sales dollar. With timely detailed information available, we had a handle on the source of our losses and insight into which orders were unprofitable. The department managers and I reviewed the daily P & L together. We discussed each loss until satisfied that we knew why it occurred and then decided on a course of action to prevent its recurrence.

The cause of a loss may have been a one-shot event, a temporary power failure, for instance, that added extra time during processing. Under such circumstances there was no need to take further action. Or the cause of a loss may have been due to complications inherent in the job. We'd watch the results when it came up again. If the loss proved repeatable, we would either find an easier and less costly way to accomplish the job, or we would raise our price and advise the customer well in advance of his next order. If, due to competitive pressures we couldn't raise the price, we might choose to abandon that business. Now at least we had the option to stanch or knowingly suffer a future loss.

As the recession worsened we were faced with a shocking development. Since our selling prices were falling due to stiffening competition, we were losing money on virtually every job we ran. How much more could we cut? In desperation we sought to increase productivity. This led to installing a team incentive system that rewarded superior worker performance. As the reader will see, it worked: in only two months both production and quality improved and our losses eased.

If a recession has no other constructive purpose, at least it forced us to identify our company's vulnerabilities and to seize perhaps our last opportunity to change old ways for the better.

Making the Most of Recession

Accountants know. But our accountant, a good one, couldn't figure out how we had turned our plummeting bottom line around. Sales were still falling. Our highly leveraged company was deep into the 1981 recession. We had refused to lay off the well-trained, dedicated people who had been with us through a long string of good years. And our spirit, despite distress all around us, remained strong and upbeat. Where was the magic?

From the time gross receipts had leveled off 18 months earlier, as a proud chief executive who never had to withdraw, I joined in battle with the marketplace. I put on additional salesmen, enhanced sales commissions, opened new territories and increased our advertising space in trade magazines. But it was a battle I had to lose. Our competition, similarly struggling to retain their share in a contracting market, had done the same.

Meanwhile, we were exhausting our working capital. I blamed the weak economy, our foolhardy competitors for quoting "below cost," confiscatory interest rates and excessive taxes. The bank, after receiving several poor back-to-back quarterly statements, cautioned me to stanch the outflow or I'd soon be in non-compliance with our loan agreement. I had to find a strategy for survival - a strategy of retreat.

First I had to acknowledge certain truths:

*As the market diminishes during a recession, it's a waste of time and money to try increasing market share. The competition becomes extremely efficient and more relentless than ever in preserving its position. No wonder I was losing the battle.

*A dollar saved goes directly to the bottom line but only a portion of a sales dollar does. Blinded by our past steady sales growth, I had looked outside for the answer, not within.

*Improving our operation either by purchasing better equipment or introducing innovative production methods or motivating employees, ultimately increases profits. Instead I made do with our old machinery, stuck with tried and true processing techniques, and cut back wages.

*The CEO is not alone. He and his employees are adrift together. Since the company's troubles affect everyone, the employees should also participate in its rescue. I had consulted no one, fearing I would lower morale still further.

I began the attack with a new approach: from 8 to 9 each morning, before the phones began ringing, a "brain trust" - a managing collective - consisting of all department heads and a weekly rotating volunteer from the rank and file, met with me as equals to formulate a coping strategy.

We made the following crucial moves:

*Abandoning our campaign to increase sales, we reverted to our original level of sales personnel and concentrated on servicing our existing accounts. It is easier to secure new business from old accounts than from accounts we hadn't yet acquired.

*Since we were principally a production organization, we would put all R & D work on hold for the duration.

*We switched to another bank where we secured a surprisingly better deal after our old bank of many years refused to grant us relief.

*We restored all hourly wages to the original level and resumed regularly scheduled increases. However, we deferred the increases to all salaried personnel until profits returned. Then they would receive what was due them over a period of weeks.

*We installed an incentive system, irrespective of profits (or losses). We began with the workers and eventually included all employees except top management.

This last move, which I shall discuss in detail in the next chapter, proved momentous.

As our good accountant perused the P & L, he observed the decrease in our sales, and administrative and supervisory expenses (as a percent of gross sales). But when he reached our labor expense, he gasped: what used to be a normal 15 percent had dropped to 10 percent (later to 5 percent). He knew now what had happened, but not how or why. That was our secret weapon!

The Managing Collective

I desperately needed ideas back in 1979. The company's progress was stalled due in large part to a slowing economy. But it was also, I felt, due to a certain apathy (even within myself), and a hardening of our ways that had developed during the organization's difficult decade of existence. It would have been easy (and expensive) to pay a management consultant to come in, learn about us, make a proposal, then walk away without any further responsibility.

It would also be defeatist. After all, I owed what success I had to applying my own resources. And I already had well-paid managers in place who knew the company better than anyone else. Had I ever asked them to take a long look beyond their own bailiwicks? Had I sought their opinion of what was wrong with our company or encouraged their suggestions on what to do about it? Aren't these the questions consultants address? It was like a dawn breaking: right under my nose, in house, were the most qualified consultants I would ever find.

We met every weekday morning in my office at 8 and quit at 9, before the phone calls began. No interruptions, except in extreme emergencies, were tolerated. Seven members of our small company of (now) fewer than 100 employees were steady attendees: the vice president of production, the first shift supervisor, the technical director, the office manager, the sales manager, a rotating production worker who participated for a week, and I. If a salesman or the visiting manager of our satellite plant happened to be in the office, he was also invited.

Our purpose was to develop new ideas and to let them fly no matter how ridiculous. Everyone had a turn to speak and if what he or she had to say wasn't completed within the hour, it was carried over to the next morning.

Though presiding, I maintained a low profile and let the group argue their thoughts freely. I only asked a question here and there or tossed out a problem with which I had been wrestling.

But this was hardly management by consensus; no vote was taken. I reserved the authority to decide which idea was worth trying. (Everyone understood that, as majority stockholder, I had the most to gain or lose.)

My first task was to break the habit most of us have of restricting our thinking to our own jobs - a natural and regrettable result imposed on us by the organizational structure. Traditionally, only the CEO sees the "big picture" and so is the one who makes the "big" decisions. Now I would make everyone a figurative CEO, place him or her in my shoes, if only for an hour a day, and perhaps in time, all day - and night. Throw a problem on the table, either big or small, and see what we can do with it collectively.

While each individual in the group had different and well-defined responsibilities, all had to put aside any claim to expertise, to superiority, and accept both criticism and ideas that concerned their departments. While we were all equal during the meeting and every opinion was respected, outside the meeting we reverted to operating within the old clearly established lines of responsibility which could not be crossed.

The unpredictable - and pleasantly surprising - member of the group was the rotating worker. That person might be a young woman from the office staff or a tough old hand from production. Understandably many workers, unaccustomed to membership in the inner sanctum and feeling intimidated sitting with the brass, only listened. However, usually by their second or third turn, encouraged by others in the same job category whose ideas were adopted, the timidity disappeared.

From these people came the practical, down-to-earth solutions that startled us by their insight. An elementary example: let's re-use our waste to purge and clean the machines between runs. Another example: there were complaints about the poor job done by an outside service that waxed the floors and cleaned the office and bathrooms. Did we know that two of our workers were once in the cleaning business and would probably be happy to do the job after hours and on weekends for their regular hourly rate? They accepted. We saved money while adding to their income. And they did a quality job for they knew precisely whom - their co-workers - they had to please.

Some workers begged off attending our meetings. They said they had nothing to contribute and had no wish to hear the problems. But they couldn't avoid hearing them. Walking through the plant I'd overhear discussions on what went on at our meetings. Most worker members, proud of their participation, were quick to spread the word to all corners of the company.

The range of creative ideas that flowed from these meetings was enormous - from hiring and firing people, to changing banks, to devising compensation plans, to seeking new markets, to establishing long-range goals and ways to achieve them and so on. The collective dealt with virtually every aspect of running the business, culminating in a series of incentive plans for all levels of the company - except top management - that ultimately eliminated most of our structural problems.

However, nothing lasts. After two years, the meetings degenerated into spurious discussions and boring recitals of petty complaints better dealt with at a lower level. Thus the group contained within itself the elements of its own demise. Owing to the collective, the company had reached a new and prosperous stage of life. Problems were its raison d'etre; without them, it lost its purpose.

Coping with Recession: An Identity Crisis

The '81 recession was still upon us and we hunkered down. Our sales and marketing manager did all the sensible things a good manager does to cope with a recession. They were steps recommended by our managing collective.

*Seeing that our competitors had become just as lean and efficient as we, he abandoned trying to increase market share.

*He cut back on advertising. In the business of manufacturing custom color concentrates for the plastics industry, advertising's effects were slow to take hold and difficult to measure.

*All new product development was put on hold. We had to conserve capital for use in operations and things certain.

*He dismissed less productive salesmen and divided their territories among our star performers.

None of this was enough. Good people still had to be laid off. Where, how could he find more business?

We had deliberately established a special niche for ourselves in an industry comprised of two major segments. Avoiding the largest segment, the big volume, low margin, commodity products, we relentlessly pursued the custom manufactured, smaller volume, high markup portion.

But in recession, rules change and niches tend to blur. Buyers depart from their traditional sources to seek lower prices. So our order-starved salesmen were pleading with management to accept the commodity business that might come their way.

The temptation to give in to their wishes was intense. A mighty argument began among the seven members of our employee collective.

We knew we were bound to lose money manufacturing low-priced commodity products. Our plant and equipment were geared to serve only our niche business. On the other hand, were our commodity-producing cousins to attempt our product line, they too would lose money.

But the issue was more fundamental than: should we or shouldn't we take in alien high-volume business at a loss? It was also an issue of pride - pride in our good reputation: the trade considered us a Cadillac caliber company. And it was an issue of identity - knowing who we were.

The collective split in two. One group (the technical director, the office manager and the maintenance supervisor) argued that to manufacture commodity products would hasten the wear and tear on our equipment and also tarnish our image. Hadn't we striven for years to attain our treasured place in the industry? Stick to who we are: "know and be thyself," even if we must lay off people, streamline the operation and wait out the bad times. Above all, don't join the commodity wolf pack and adopt its supermarket mentality.

I found it an especially powerful argument. It had been my guide from the day I became chief executive 13 years earlier. I took enormous pride in having helped to create a quality company in an industry where most of our competitors still hadn't mastered the skill of turning out consistently good product. Having been trained in a large corporation that eventually made itself all things to all customers, I had witnessed the disaster that resulted and learned the danger of forgetting one's niche.

The other group (the sales manager, the production manager and the accountant) advanced equally convincing reasons why we should take on marginal business. It would boost the morale of our salesmen whose income was in part based on commission. In offering our customers a more complete product line, we would be shutting out desperate commodity producers who were trying to invade our market. With more volume we'd have no need to lay off trained workers and risk losing them. The accountant declared that were we to change our costing assumptions, even though our margins would be thinner than customary, losses needn't occur.

Vacillating between both views, I recalled the accountant's argument as the rationale behind my former employer's adoption of their commodity strategy. By assuming all overhead costs were absorbed by profitable custom products, then only direct costs (material, labor, electricity, wear and tear and shipping) need be applied to the new low-margin items. Viewing it another way, if overhead were assigned to the cost of commodity products, then the overall overhead cost for all products would be reduced. The logic was irrefutable.

But, it didn't work. In time the commodity portion of that company's product mix gathered its own momentum and overwhelmed the more profitable segment. Eventually it even interfered with scheduling and led to lost orders. Gradually the company ceased to be the profitable company it had been; it had lost its original identity.

I proposed a compromise to the collective. Our salesmen could pursue a limited amount of commodity business at competitive prices. However, we would produce commodity items only to inventory - not to meet specific customer requests - in order not to jeopardize our usual excellent servicing of profitable customers. No custom order would be sacrificed for a commodity order.

But we must be wary and not delude ourselves. We must acknowledge the two types of business are in conflict. All products, custom and commodity, must carry their share of overhead costs. All employees must understand that the company would lose money on every commodity pound it sold. Most important, all employees must understand we did this to remain as intact as possible while waiting for the sick economy to get well. It worked - but for only a year.

Leadership and Trust

At a conference of communications specialists (at which I was a guest speaker) who promote dissemination of information within their companies, the interviewer asked, "What message would you give to help us do our jobs better?" In almost knee-jerk reaction I replied: "Get to your CEO. Persuade him of the importance of free communication and openness. A company is strictly a mirror of the CEO's personality and style. His employees march in lockstep to his wishes. Without his support and belief in what you're doing, you'll be fighting a losing battle."

During the coffee break that followed, one of the attendees, an employee of an American blue chip company, was heard to say, "But my CEO is elusive. When he arrives in the morning he slips into a private elevator that takes him to his office where he remains secluded all day. I can't reach him."

The audience listened to my story. By the time the size of our company reached 100 employees, I too was as unapproachable as that corporate CEO. My contacts were limited to no more than a half dozen key people. No one knew the details of what was happening in the rest of the company, small though it was, beyond their own departments. Certainly no one in the company was privy to its financials or even to costs that pertained to their own bailiwicks.

Though I was allegedly their trusted leader, I withheld from my employees facts that would reveal their specific contribution to the success or failure of the company's performance. Since I believed knowledge is power, I also believed that by divulging so-called confidential information I would be diminished and made vulnerable. I clung to secrecy as if my life depended on it. And I maintained a distance from the rank-and-file, issuing proclamations through key people and the bulletin board. When we were doing well, I played it down and when we were doing badly, God forbid I should admit it. In short, I followed the traditional pattern of most CEOs of closely held businesses.

Then came the onset of the 1981-1982 recession, the worst post-war decline to that date. After struggling in vain for a year to counteract declining sales and bottom-line losses, I realized I would have to level with my employees and confess my failure. At this point, I also questioned my ability as their leader. After all, I was self-appointed, their CEO by dint of my willingness to take a risk in business and their need for jobs. Indeed, to put it bluntly, I was a dictator, perhaps one confined to a small universe, but the power with which the employees had to reckon. Nor did the organizational structure offer them the opportunity to wield much power of their own. We had no union.

I felt opening up the company, especially showing our financials, could be dangerous and unreasonable demands might follow. But I was willing to gamble that once everyone saw the company's plight, the employees would pitch in to help me solve it. In other words, by demonstrating my trust in them, they would offer their trust in return. That's precisely what happened. They redoubled their personal efforts on the job and postponed wage increases without complaint. Most important, they offered a stream of innovative ideas to keep us alive through the crisis.

At the conference a questioner asked, "What led you to open up the company?" I replied, of course, it was the recession. But that's only partly true. Beneath that fact was my human longing to trust and not be alone. It's macho to suffer, to show no vulnerability as proof of one's manhood. But I discovered something marvelous. As the employees and I, due to the new openness, entered a silent pact of faith and trust, I felt powerful again. What's more, the threat of losing that power was gone. Even if we failed - and we certainly didn't - I would have triumphed. Our company had become a single entity in which all were motivated by mutual consent. It was an experience I had only once before - on the other side of a relationship.

It happened during World War II. I was just out of high school and a lowly member of a Seabee battalion (the Naval Construction Battalions). We were assigned to building docks, roads and airstrips in the South Pacific. As soon as our outfit debarked at Hollandia, New Guinea, the officers located a choice spot by the shore of Humbolt Bay and ordered the enlisted men to construct officers' quarters (BOQ), including a private dining room and showers.

When Joe Nowell, our handsome, charismatic, hot-tempered Commander got wind of this, he burst into a rage. It was rumored he threw his chair across his desk and out of his tent. He rescinded his officers' orders and had us build our own quarters first. The enlisted men came before the brass, he declared. The enlisted men were the producers. Whether the officers liked it or not, he insisted they live with the enlisted men in their quarters until all the latter's needs were met.

After that episode, we adored our commander and would go to any length to please him. Indeed, as we worked around the clock, Commander Nowell would appear at all hours, even at 3 A.M. He praised us for pulling together in building the base. Obviously the officers despised him - but they never failed to do his bidding. He commanded their respect if not their love.

Until that incident Commander Nowell was merely the appointed leader, just as I, the CEO, was self-appointed. In him I had a model of a true leader. He earned the loyalty and trust of his men by showing his trust and belief in their importance and concern for their welfare. Without my realizing it, he had shown me the way.

Preserving Brain Power

The question is painful: Who in a company is expendable when hard times strike? The answer depends on how you see the future. Is the company experiencing only a temporary setback? Or is something more fundamental happening that calls for a permanent downsizing of the company?

Many CEOs are often slow to face unpleasant realities, especially when they've been at the helm during years of smooth sailing. Forgetting that our economy is inherently cyclical, CEOs may be lulled into complacency. For almost two years I couldn't decide what long-term effect, if any, the recession of the early '80s would have on our company.

At first we viewed our sales decline as temporary. It would only be a matter of months, we thought, before a rebound occurred. We'd hold on and thank our lucky stars no one in management need be let go. In the meantime, with workers laid off, the supervisors and department heads found themselves with little to do. They spent most of their time trying to keep busy with trivial matters and commiserating with each other over their boredom. Meanwhile the bottom line was hemorrhaging. Eventually reality forced me to acknowledge the truth. We could no longer afford a full-size corps of supervisors and executives - the brains of the organization - that had taken years of trial and error to assemble.

Difficult though it was, I had to concede the possibility our company would have to remain smaller for the forseeable future. Each of our key people had an income equivalent to two or three ordinary workers combined. Letting them go would be the quickest and easiest way to cut expenses.

I summoned our entire supervisory and executive staff to a meeting. The salesmen, who found our customers no busier than we, were also called off the road to attend. I informed everyone of our plight and announced that some of them would have to leave unless we could devise an alternative.

Sure enough, obviously motivated to save their jobs, they came up with a two-part solution. The first step was a temporary substantial salary reduction. Once the bottom line recovered, I suggested that salaries would be restored to the original amounts plus a gradual payout of the accumulated difference. There were naturally some holdouts who refused to sacrifice. Their relationship with the company was never the same again.

The second part was more dramatic. The executives would remove their ties and white shirts, don worker's clothes and do whatever work had to be done. They would replace laid off workers, or fill in for those on vacation. More often they would simply pitch in when a spate of incoming orders became too much for our skeleton crew of workers to handle. Obviously, by placing inexperienced people in blue-collar jobs a certain degree of efficiency had to be compromised. But, as it turned out, the experiment was more successful than we expected.

Since our production supervisors and foremen had come from the ranks, they already had the necessary experience to man our machinery. In a very short time they again became as adept as the workers they replaced. As for the other department heads who performed less skilled tasks such as operating a forklift, helping in maintenance or weighing out formulas, they were cumbersome on the job at first. But they learned their jobs quickly and amazingly well. Their morale rebounded. They instituted improvements. Why not? These people were our best and brightest.

Instead of making fruitless sales calls the salesmen spent part of their time contacting more customers by phone and helping with office chores. Working in the plant, they learned more about how our products were made (and the problems involved) than they had during all the previous years of their employment. This was just one surprise benefit from our experiment.

And there were others. When the rebound finally came we were transformed into a more efficient company than before the recession. Plant procedures had been improved upon. Our key people had a more cooperative spirit since they could now appreciate what the workers had to contend with every day. And most importantly, after experiencing a crisis and pulling together there was a closer feeling among us. After all, we had come through a difficult period without losing a single valuable person. As CEO this I found most gratifying.

Of course it could have gone the other way. The rebound could have taken years to happen. Then we would have lost many of these people. Nobody with managerial skills finds challenge in driving a forklift forever. When talented people are lost, they are usually lost forever to their new employer. In a sense, luck was part three of our two-part solution. In the slow recovery of '91-'92 we might not have fared so well.

Recession Proofing a Company's Employees

When I first read that many Japanese companies guaranteed their employees lifetime employment, I couldn't decide whether to admire them for their courage or deride them for their foolhardiness. How could a company possibly expect to weather a recession and not lay off a portion of its people? (However, it is true the Japanese economy appears not to be as cyclical as ours.)

During three recessions, laying off our people was standard operating procedure, mandatory, a common American custom. After all, when business activity is insufficient to keep everyone occupied and to maintain the bottom line at its accustomed (or survival) level, it is only natural the company cut back its personnel, typically the most costly and vulnerable expense item in the P & L. Moreover, how does one lay off a machine or a building or a bank loan?

Still, though layoffs seemed logical and necessary, they were always the most distasteful and painful decision we managers - including myself - ever had to make. Our company was small enough - reduced to 50 employees by then - and our turnover infrequent enough that everybody knew everybody else by first name, regardless of rank. Indeed, most of us were familiar with the details of each other's personal lives: how many kids a worker supported, whose were in college, who was saving for a down payment on a new house, which families were beset with illness.

Additionally painful was the necessity of having to lay off trained, proven, highly motivated people who were simply victims of economic forces beyond their - and management's - control. Most of us felt helpless and outraged at being punished for having done nothing wrong.

But were we - workers and management alike - really helpless? Were we not submitting to circumstances rather than trying to control them? What then is the alternative to a recession driven layoff? The foolhardy Japanese solution, a commitment to lifetime employment? There's a surefire prescription for disaster. Right?

Or is it? After each of three recessions (roughly one every four years) we countered with the usual layoffs, several excellent workers failed to return when business improved. Replacing competent and trained employees with green people was, of course, inconvenient - and costly. But worse, it delayed the restoration of our pre-recession efficiency just when we needed it most to meet the unpredictable order pattern of a turnaround. (Since our product formulations were proprietary we hesitated to subcontract work out.)

It was evident that our most valuable human asset was not the hands but the brains seasoned by long experience. This principle also applied to returning laid-off employees who, having lost touch with their jobs, were out of practice. If layoffs make economic sense in bad times, they have a strikingly adverse effect as good times return.

Though laid-off employees were thrilled at being called back, we often observed a residual bitterness in their attitude, especially after they saw that certain others remained on the job through the tough time. Subtle though it was, those employees seemed less secure and committed than before the layoff. If returning employees didn't ask the boss, they had to ask themselves: How long will it be before the next layoff? With this question implanted, when slow times returned - a guaranteed event - our formerly laid-off employees sought to protect themselves against the dreaded layoff notice by the only tactical means at their disposal: a slowdown.

In prior crises we often broke from the bounds of conventional thinking by seeking the solution in a condition precisely opposite the one troubling us. We called this the Lesson of the Opposite, a most fruitful creative technique, similar in effectiveness to the Five Whys of lean production. We used it here, to wit: If laying off is the problem then perhaps working overtime, it's opposite, is the answer.

As good times returned, hesitating to hire more hands until we were sure the gathering sales momentum would last, we asked people to work overtime. At the beginning they were not only willing, but eager to cooperate. Eventually, flushed after a period of substantial weekly paychecks, many refused and we would fail to meet delivery commitments. If a layoff was hard on the employee, an employee's rejection of overtime was hard on management. It meant missed opportunities for the company and unhappy customers. Consequently we hired additional people, some of whom, when the cycle reversed, inevitably had to be laid off.

(Having no union, we laid off less according to seniority and more according to performance.) Round and round it went.

Sales were nearing a peak. We held a plant-wide meeting before hiring more people and offered the workers a proposal gleaned from our Lesson of the Opposite: Would the employees work any necessary overtime, and perform any reasonable job request in exchange for the company's promise to eliminate all future layoffs? If so, the company would delay hiring additional people until the first signs of genuine weariness appeared. Being in a cyclical business, everyone, especially management, knew we had made a daring offer. The employees went for it without hesitation.

But we had a few aces to play just in case we were caught short-handed. By using our sales history, plus a factor for growth to define the sales range from the depths of recession to the heights of prosperity, we estimated how many employees we would need in various functions to maintain efficient productivity within those limits. And we had some escape valves too. When we found ourselves straining under pressure to produce, we called in retirees who were delighted to come to our rescue and mix with the gang again. For the summer, our busiest season, we hired bright college students who caught on quickly. And we called on agencies that specialized in temporary experienced help for people who could perform our routine tasks.

We were also ready for the day sales would sag. As that condition developed we busied our people by expanding our inventory of standard items - maintained at minimum as the good times matured - to an established maximum. We assigned anyone not kept busy with his or her regular task, even foremen and supervisors, to maintenance projects intentionally delayed for such an occasion. These could range from cleaning and painting the exterior or interior of the building to rebuilding worn equipment as preventive maintenance.

Most important was the willingness of everyone for the sake of security to pitch in and do whatever job was needed. This led, in time, to retraining everyone to do one or more jobs. There was also another reason. After a year an employee received one week's vacation, five years two weeks, 10 years three weeks, 15 years four weeks. During slowdowns, idle employees were urged to use part of their paid vacations. Most did, especially those with substantial seniority. It worked marvelously.

Employee morale attained a new height; turnover already low, became negligible. Pride in being a part of a caring organization was clearly evident. A desire to exert extra effort on the company's behalf became the norm. With transients no longer in our midst, we had, in a sense, become a stable, cohesive "family." Though we endured two more recessions, one serious, before the company was sold, we never had another layoff in the eight years that followed.

And there were other unanticipated pluses. By eliminating layoffs and reducing the number of permanent employees enrolled, we reduced our generous benefit costs. Perhaps our major triumph was the drastic reduction of our financial contribution to the state's unemployment pool. Somehow, reducing our involuntary contribution to government seemed, at least to this CEO, the most satisfying fallout of all.

My Worst Mistakes in Business

Looking back over almost 20 years as CEO, I can state, without hesitation, the toughest decisions I had to make concerned laying off or firing people. Yet, not laying people off and not firing those who proved unsuitable, were the most costly mistakes I ever made. Though inherently a mover, I was expert at procrastination in such matters. Compared to people decisions, deciding whether to add to the building, install another production line or expand the sales force, all of which involved much more money and risk, was a breeze. Depriving a person of his or her livelihood, and, in a sense, his or her self-respect, no matter for how brief a time, is the "dirtiest" task anyone in authority - and with a conscience - has to face.

The dilemma applies more to small companies than to large corporations. Decision makers at the headquarters of a far-flung company are sufficiently removed from the flesh and blood consequences of their actions to feel many pangs of guilt. From a strictly bottom-line point of view this is just as well. I had often wished I had a similar luxury.

But, in our small company in which I was on a first-name basis with all of our employees, the bottom line was only one consideration, and often the last one. I so consistently broke my own rule never to hire friends and relatives, it was a joke. How could I turn down someone in need of a job and of whom I was fond? To lay them off or fire them had to be sacrilegious. I convinced myself each case would be an exception - even though, given time, it proved otherwise.

Typically, we waited until we were in desperate straits before laying off people. Of course, this was far too late. Long before we made the fateful decision, we knew what we should have been doing. The situation won't last, we rationalized, and pretended the adverse bottom line would go away - sooner or later. Eventually, driven by our collective pain and suffering, we found a way to eliminate layoffs during hard times by trading our employees' willingness to work overtime in good times for our desire to keep the roster consistently lean, especially during slowdowns.

Dismissing people is far more earthshaking. Since it's permanent, or should be, it's also emotionally charged - for all concerned. I have previously described the unhappy episodes with my wife's capable cousin, the young salesman, and with the relative who, reaching his 60s, eased off. I have also written about the loss of our first Technical Director, the genius, who contributed much but couldn't grow with the job.

In our company, the position of Technical Director had the most turnover. Another of our TD's had a Ph.D. He was gentle and kind and a bird watcher. Though he was brilliant in technical matters, he was unable to discriminate in dealing with customers between what was confidential and and what was not. We agonized over him because firing a bird watcher has to be a despicable act. Nevertheless after he had inadvertently revealed our costs and formulations, we had no choice.

Our most momentous separation involved an exceptionally talented TD who, for the five years he was with us, chronically complained about his lot in life. He complained not only to me, but also to anyone within earshot. Still, he was so capable and ran his department so efficiently I put up with him. One day he announced he was leaving. Though he had become attached to us, he felt it was time to move on - unless I was willing to meet the would-be employer's terms. While he saw a greener pasture across the street, from our vantage point he was swapping us for a brown, weedy lot. We let him walk.

Then a surprising thing happened. Everyone noticed, myself included, that suddenly a new lightness pervaded the atmosphere as if a great weight had been lifted. Unbeknownst to us, we had shared his burden of dissatisfaction for five years. A new, happy spirit reigned. It was startling.

Why hadn't I gotten rid of him years before? I had always dreaded listening to his constant litany of complaints. Why had I ignored my instincts? But better later than not at all. In less than two years, unhappy with his employer, he asked to return. He realized he had been happy with us all along. I turned him down, convinced it was not us, nor even his current employer, with whom he was miserable. It was himself.

In no instance after we let a person go did that person fail to find another job. In fact, our ex-employee usually found more happiness elsewhere. In every instance we found ourselves better off. The lesson learned: what's best for the company is best for the employee is likely to be best for the company. That includes firing as well as hiring the employee. It took years before I understood this simple precept. Having the wrong person in a job, for whatever reason, is a business blunder of the first order.

CHAPTER VI

EXPERIMENTS IN MOTIVATION

What's Wrong with Profit Sharing?

How could anyone knock profit sharing? Even companies that don't have such a plan admit that in principle it's not a bad idea. After all, aren't profits the motivating force driving entrepreneurs? Even the less entrepreneurial managements of large corporations respond to it. But can we assume, as many American and Japanese corporations do, that profits are also the motivating force driving the ordinary production or staff worker?

What would happen if a company were to drop its profit sharing plan? Would productivity decline? Is there a more effective way to motivate people? Our company came up with some answers.

We introduced a profit sharing plan (taxes were deferred until cashing in) at a company-wide meeting with much hoopla and high expectations. Each year the company would contribute an arbitrary sum from its profits to the plan. But the first year turned out to be a bad one. So infinitesimal was the bottom line that the distribution most employees received was an insult. The second year was better, but hardly cause for euphoria. At meetings held each year-end, management held out the hope, if not the promise, things would get better due to certain steps we had outlined. By the third year, conditions had so improved the contribution was significant for everybody.

Still, the question remained: wouldn't we have done just as well without a profit sharing plan? Instead of using our bottom line as a gauge for "improvement," perhaps measuring our productivity - in our case the average hourly production rate - would reveal whether profit was indeed a motivating factor. (Our Incentive Plan hadn't yet been born.) The result: it wasn't. Our production rates before and after contributing to the plan were the same. Yet we were reluctant to take away any benefit - a wise policy as many CEO's know. Instead, realizing most Americans have a penchant for immediate gratification, we speculated that distributing profits in cash each quarter addresses that inclination and provides incentive. We acknowledged this was somewhat risky. After all, a quarter might be profitable, but we could well end up the year in the red.

This step resulted in an unanticipated disaster.

Being a closely held company, we would not reveal the bottom line to our employees. They had to take our word for it. For the first two quarters we were sufficiently profitable to provide everyone with a substantial bonus. But in the third quarter we lost money - no bonus. Though everyone was disappointed, they were also philosophical. Then, in the fourth quarter, we broke even - no bonus again, and we ended the year slightly in the black. But this time the reaction was downright hostile: rumors abounded management had falsified the bottom line.

The traditional adversarial monster of labor/management distrust had surfaced. We would have been better off if we had dropped profit sharing entirely rather than modified it. Management, including myself of course, was outraged. Being a product of the free enterprise system, I subscribed to the principle that with risk sometimes you win and sometimes you lose. Success is rarely a straight line up. But our employees, though taking no risk, expected only to share in profits and not suffer losses - or, as in this case, stay even.

We declared cash quarterly profit sharing a failure and returned to our old system of granting bonuses at year-end only to key people. This hardly promoted trust between the rank-and-file and management, nor motivated either to assist the other in attaining its goals. Not until a recession struck years later, and the company was in crisis, did we discover the formula that would lead to mutual cooperation and trust. During the downturn profit sharing was a moot issue anyway since we had few profits to share.

The solution, we learned, was to tie reward to productivity, not profits. By its very nature this impacts the bottom line for better or worse. But improvement didn't guarantee profits. Our earlier mistake was we assumed everybody, workers and management alike, were directly responsible for bottom-line performance.

How responsible were the workers? Hadn't their level of productivity depended on management's skill and not the other way around? Had the workers participated in developing marketing strategy, in designing products, in raising capital, in innovating processing methods, in creating a smooth running organization, in bringing to the business a style and spirit essential to its success? Certainly not, though why they hadn't will be discussed later. The workers' role was contingent upon management's expertise, and only partially and conditionally connected to profits (or losses).

What worked, and worked consistently, was a team incentive system that satisfied our people's need for immediate gratification. It was entirely autonomous and based strictly on performance; profits were irrelevant. It was assumed the bottom line was the measure of only management's performance. Were we to allow everyone to join management in making policy decisions, especially those affecting their immediate concerns, they too should share in the bottom line. Under these conditions they would be sufficiently informed to know the road to profitability is no joy ride. That's what eventually happened - much to our good fortune.

The Birth of An Incentive Plan that Works

The company was still dead in the water. All growth plans were off. Our bottom line had been hovering around break-even for two years. Worried we might start sinking, the Managing Collective and I decided to turn our gaze from the erratic world outside, to the more manageable one within - to ourselves.

We asked: how can we run the company better, fatten the bottom line, improve individual performance, provide more security?

Introduce innovative methods, utilize better equipment, suggested our snappy production V.P. OK, what specifically did he have in mind? Silence.

Our solicitous female office manager asked: aren't human beings really at the core of a business's success or failure?

The discussion was joined.

How do people get other people to do better?

Praise.

As a benevolent autocracy we were already doing that by means of token awards and kudos posted on the bulletin board.

Better wages.

Though we were a non-union company, our wages were deliberately close to our unionized competitors' and we offered more benefits.

Reward?

Maybe, but not the traditional meager reward most companies offer to motivate their people. How about something achievable, substantial and immediate? Who could possibly resist, say, the possibility of increasing his or her paycheck by 20 to 25 percent each month - enough to pay the rent?

We focussed on productivity. Since our workers' productivity constituted the essence of our profitability, we devised their incentive plan first.

Any improvement in production would have to be directly measurable. And to measure performance we established a base line for comparison's sake: the historical average hourly output per production line. To put it generically, the average number of widgets we had produced per hour on a widget machine for the last five years. Since the rate was amazingly consistent, we knew our manufacturing cost per widget. Any increase in the production rate reduced that cost and generated a specific sum of extra dollars - that we wouldn't have made otherwise - to be divided between the company and the workers directly involved. A suitable ratio, we decided, would be one part to the worker, two parts to the company.

At month's end, after calculating the difference between the improved rate and the historical rate, we posted each production line's results on the cafeteria bulletin board. We included the bonus sum (arrived at by a simple formula) due each team. Thus, with monetary reward came recognition. The members of the top team were, at least for a month, the acknowledged pros.

The team?

Several interdependent steps were necessary to produce a widget. Each required special skills in several departments and across all shifts. We defined a member of a particular team as anyone who was directly involved in a specific way with a particular production line, regardless of department or shift. Those departments that serviced all lines, shipping and receiving for example, or maintenance, received an incentive reward based on the average gain for all teams combined. Therefore, it was in those departments' interest to contribute whatever they could to the efficiency of every line and every worker.

Since reward was given for team, and not individual effort, cooperation between workers superseded competition. An unanticipated benefit surfaced. The slackers, those who couldn't or wouldn't produce at the pace the team set, quit under intense social pressure. When the remaining team members asked that we not hire replacements for those who quit as fewer members meant greater individual reward - we were skeptical. But the teams soon became so efficient and self-regulating that even supervision became unnecessary.

Some of our foremen and supervisors, finding themselves superfluous and bored, went for the money and became workers themselves. Others were transferred to our new midwest satellite. Not only had the incentive improved productivity, it also reduced portions of our fixed costs.

The effect on the bottom line was dramatic. In a few months we attained the 20 percent increase in production we had originally envisioned. But quality problems developed. Simply increasing the production of widgets wasn't enough. They had to be perfect widgets accurately meeting customer's specifications. Since our people weren't gods (or Japanese) they were bound to make mistakes and produce defective widgets. No complaint if this happens only once in a while and we keep it in the family. But the bad widgets better not get out the door and into customers' hands.

Meet the negative incentive. Every widget could be traced to the team that made it through an ID (lot) number. The cost of restoring or replacing widgets returned by a customer would be deducted from the responsible team's future reward. Quality improved so that returns, once at a 1 percent level, became negligible.

We coasted for a few more months, pleased with ourselves. Then the worker member of our management collective revealed we could expect still better performance - under one condition. What condition? That we do not tamper with the original base line, the historical average we had established. Usually when performance improves, doesn't management revise the norm as justification for eliminating or reducing the reward?

Astonished, we asked the worker whether our people had been taking it easy those past years. The worker's reply: They had never been given reason to produce more than management expected. Thus it had been a failure of management, not the workers. Immediately I had posted on the bulletin board, and in a notice placed in every pay envelope, my signed promise that under no circumstances (except for a change in equipment or process) would the base line be altered as long as I remained CEO. The original average would remain sacrosanct. That's all the teams needed to know.

During the next two years our roster of 100 employees fell at one point to only 35. But, hard to believe but true, they produced 50 percent more output than that of our pre-incentive era.

The team incentive demonstrated how powerful such a plan, unshackled from profits, could be. Therein lay the magic. We introduced a similar plan into every department (the office, the lab, maintenance, shipping, even middle management) and went on to unprecedented heights of profitability.

Can we conclude from this that American workers are, to put it politely, apathetic and lazy? Or should we conclude they're merely reacting to management's shortsighted greed and cynical unwillingness to reward?

A Description of an Incentive Plan
That Works
(Reward For Excellence)

A squad of Japanese appeared in the lobby early one morning. They were among dozens of lookers who had considered buying our company. They came bearing gifts for our executives: gold cuff links engraved with their giant company's logo. Though they didn't buy, we knew they were impressed. As they left they announced in unison: "Just like Japanese company." But we weren't; they failed to detect the difference.

What they saw as they toured our plant were teams of enthusiastic workers moving swiftly about as if time were the enemy. In our office they saw a staff so engrossed in what they were doing they barely noticed the presence of visitors. And when I invited our guests to speak to a worker, the employee's response always began with a smile.

We were an open company operating under the influence of team incentives and in a business culture in many respects not unlike that at Toyota. Except we had taken that culture further: our workers participated in making management policy decisions as well as decisions affecting their own bailiwicks. Everyone owned "a piece of the action," and everyone was familiar with (and taught to understand) every detail of our quarterly P & L.

We acknowledged the wisdom of Taiichi Ohno of Toyota. He discovered the enormous advantages of cooperative team effort and free group expression. But we felt, due to our peculiarly American penchant for competitiveness and individuality, the team approach was not enough. Unlike the patient Japanese, who seek lifetime security, our impatient people are reward oriented and seek immediate gratification. Thus we put an American spin on the team concept: we added an incentive system. But it wasn't typical.

The Fundamental Features of an Incentive Plan

*A plan's aim is the improvement in productivity and quality.

*The improvement must be measurable.

*The reward depends solely on the desired improvement irrespective of profitability.

*The reward is based on 1) the rate increase in the average number of units produced by a team over a specific period or 2) the savings engendered as a result of a team's specific action.

*The reward is given to the team and divided among members according to the number of days each worked.

*The reward is "immediate," at least monthly (except for middle management whose performance is best measured quarterly).

*The reward must be potentially substantial enough to pay an employee's monthly rent or more.

*The team's composition is logically based on related functions or a specific common result. This promotes cooperation and discourages competition between individuals. It crosses shifts.

*The team controls the function or operational end result for which it receives reward.

*Results are measured against a "base line" derived from an historical average.

*The company must guarantee that the base line remain sacrosanct (unless there's an equipment or process change).

*A negative incentive for poor quality (that which goes out the door) is applied against future reward.

*Absenteeism negatively affects only individual reward, not the team's.

*The size of the team is determined by its members. It can reduce its number so long as its efficiency is not compromised.

*Reward is based on team results, not team size.

*The company apportions the dollars saved due to increased productivity between the team and itself - no more than one to one, no less than one third for the employees.

*The company posts monthly for all to see each team's and each member's incentive reward.

*To avoid possible employee burnout, the company provides frequent time off - a generous vacation policy.

(See the Appendix for how to compute a hypothetical incentive system.)

Before introducing the team incentive plant-wide, we presented it to a small four-member department for a three month trial period. If either the team or management was dissatisfied, the company could revise the plan to our mutual satisfaction or abandon it.

Both sides were cautious. The inherent suspicion between the American worker and his boss hovered like a ghost over our discussions. The team feared that if they showed what they could really do, the incentive would be dropped and they would still be held to their increased rate.

Management, always trying to maximize gain, feared that were the team to increase productivity beyond its estimate, the reward would be excessive, even get out of hand.

Yet we put aside our reservations and chose to gamble together. I notified all employees of what we were about. Then everyone waited and watched. From the moment the first month's bonus figures were posted, the plan sold itself. The rest of the plant begged to be put on incentive. As soon as we could develop the statistical evidence and devise a measurable base and reward that fit each department, we extended it.

The performance of some departments, such as shipping and maintenance, was difficult to measure. They received an incentive based on the performance of a combination of teams which depended on their services - in effect where they could make a contribution and were a controlling factor. Since it behooved these departments to keep the teams running smoothly, they surely did. This is discussed at more length below.

We tied the office staff's incentive to a reduction in the amount of supplies it consumed and the phone bill. (Phone small talk decreased noticeably and we bought a new copier that used cheaper paper.) Middle management was rewarded quarterly according to how effectively it could bring down overhead costs. The purchasing agent's bonus depended on how well inventory levels and raw material costs were reduced below earlier normal levels.

Within a couple of years the entire operation was on incentive, except for the CEO whose reward was the gift of negligible turnover, a corps of loyal, contented employees, a smooth running business and unprecedented profits.

So Team Incentives Are Un-American

We weren't surprised when our team incentive system improved productivity - though it far exceeded expectations. And we weren't surprised when a negative incentive for allowing defective goods to land in a customer's hands improved quality. But we never expected to face a new set of problems and challenges.

The first problem arrived early on. Of the six employees that comprised the team, one was far superior to the others and one was hopelessly inept and unable to keep up. Everyone was carrying the laggard and the outstanding worker, by contributing more than the others, was receiving an insufficient share of the reward.

We expected to encourage cooperation between employees under the assumption that teamwork as opposed to individual competition would promote efficiency. But we were aware the team approach was inconsistent with our culture in which individualism is paramount, reward goes to the winner, and mediocrity is often coddled.

We waited, hoping the team would deal with its own crisis. After a while the social pressure on the poor performer led to his departure. Since the fewer the members of a team, the greater the reward per member, the remaining members asked that he not be replaced. This, of course, worked only to a point. Exhaustion - burnout - did eventually result.

As for the inequity in reward concerning the best worker, we abandoned our traditional policy of paying everyone the same hourly pay for performing the same task. No longer could we ignore the fact some people simply do certain things better than other people and should be compensated accordingly. The team had to recognize this truth. After all, every member was now the beneficiary of the superior worker's excellence. The team easily accepted the advancement of the superior worker to a higher hourly pay grade. It was a trade-off for the extra earnings all received from that worker's labor. Moreover, that worker no longer felt he was pulling more than his own weight.

After a few months, just as the new arrangement seemed to be going smoothly, the team had a few minor accidents in which injuries resulted. We also observed a small decline in the production rate. Clearly the team was exhausting itself, approaching burnout. Should we tell it, against instinct and every management principle, to slow down?

We solved the problem by means of a liberal vacation policy, (one year=one week; two years=two weeks; five years=three weeks; 15 years=four weeks; and most were five-year-plus employees). We insisted each worker take a one or two-week portion off at reasonably spaced intervals through the year. And we encouraged job switching. This necessitated, of course, that each team member know the other's job, a given when we established the program.

The next problem was with ourselves as managers. Though we were paying a substantial bonus each month, the company was still operating either in the red or near break-even. Paying more when you're not making it is hard to take. Wouldn't it be more appropriate to tie rewards to profits rather than productivity? But it remained that the incentive was providing value. In this instance we had to stop thinking short-term, a view both rational and necessary when things are going badly.

We realized any incentive related to profit is neither direct nor immediate, two important ingredients in motivating people. Furthermore, how responsible is a worker for a company's profits? We had to understand the bottom line is directly the result of management's actions, not the workers'. Only through management's policies and by its standards, do the workers' efforts affect profits. Once we perceived this we were at peace with the creature we had created.

The success of the incentive system, of which the team's monetary results were posted on the bulletin board each month for all to envy, led to our next problem: every department clamored to be similarly rewarded. But not all functions were measurable and did not lend themselves to an incentive system. Nevertheless, we investigated the possibility of introducing some kind of reward system based on improved performance for every possible team. We were amazed to discover no employee need be left out.

The productivity of some departments, say shipping and receiving or maintenance, was hard to evaluate. However, the success of these ancillary units was related to the performance of the primary sections. They were, in a sense, symbiotic. The job of maintenance, for instance, was to keep production's equipment operating smoothly. The job of shipping and receiving was to keep production supplied with raw materials from an orderly inventory and to remove finished goods from the production floor and arrange for prompt shipment to the customer. Why not then tie the incentive of such groups to that of the departments which they served? (Shipping's and maintenance's incentive can be additionally tied to savings in their departmental expenses.) We did and it worked: by rewarding cooperation among inter-dependent functions it expanded the team spirit, integrating it into a larger entity.

What about management which was directly responsible for profits? Of course, when profits are nil or lean, profit sharing is worthless as a motivator. But we searched and found another way to measure management's effectiveness: return on capital. Though there may be no return during an unprofitable year, the factors contributing to its enhancement, or the opposite, prevail nevertheless.

For example, our purchasing department's effectiveness was measured by its ability to control raw material inventory. Less inventory required less working capital resulting in lower interest cost. The purchasing department was also rewarded for minimizing raw material costs - a measure of their bargaining ability. We related the reward of the office staff to a reduction in their use of office supplies and other factors over which they had control such as the phone bill. The production supervisors' rewards were related to the combined rewards of the departments under them. And higher managements' bonuses depended strictly on total return on invested capital. The staff and management received rewards that covered longer periods, usually a quarter or longer.

Needless to say, profits followed - even as sales declined during the deepening slowdown. The entire company was on incentive, operating as a single team. But there was more to do: our next step was to concern ourselves with the individual within the team. Despite incentives, not everyone was satisfied. And we were reconciled that not everyone would be. Still, it was worth a try to aim for happiness: we began preference testing, another successful experiment.

Recognition Versus Monetary Reward

A quick review. There were two ways we could improve our declining bottom line: increase sales without increasing overhead and/or increase productivity. But during the recession when demand for our products was falling, increasing sales was a near impossibility. By default, we had to find a way to increase the rate of output (productivity) while at the same time reduce the work force consistent with the drop in orders. We concluded that reward for extra effort was the way to go.

In the 16 years I had worked for other companies, some large and publicly owned, some small and closely held, I encountered none that offered a reward for extra effort. The most one could expect was a year-end bonus, an annual pay increase, or advancement to a better paying job within the company. All are not to be denigrated. Though these rewards constituted a form of recognition for doing my job well, in no case did I have a say in whether I would receive a reward. Certainly I had no control over the magnitude of any reward. The entire matter was subject to the whim of my boss and his boss and depended somewhat on how well they liked me.

As an entrepreneur, I clearly knew what motivated me: money - but not money by itself. It was money earned from freely applying my ingenuity, my intelligence and my courage. Money, then, was the ultimate form of recognition and a measure of my proficiency. It made me feel good that what I had to offer had value.

Not until I retired and began writing did I become aware of the deeper significance of monetary reward. No matter how much praise my articles and stories might elicit from friends or editors who chose not to publish them, I remained unimpressed until someone plunked down cash. Only then could I be sure what I had written was appreciated.

As for our employees, I wouldn't assume they possessed the entrepreneurial instinct. But I felt safe in assuming that, like any entrepreneur, they would welcome the opportunity to increase their income by their own effort, and have control over doing so. The control factor is the major distinction between recognition and an incentive bonus. The incentive places responsibility squarely on the achiever. The employee is freed of the uncertainty, and possibly the bias, of management's judgement.

Not that recognition is to be ignored as a motivator. We combined recognition with the bonus by posting the incentive results on the cafeteria bulletin board for all to see. The posting of the reward signified management's appreciation of superior performance. It was the company crowing over the success of its best teams. Nor was reward judgemental. The figures were earned and spoke for themselves. The message was: anybody can do it if they want to try.

How effective is an incentive reward at higher management levels - at the level of the top brass, including the CEO? Are rewards even necessary to motivate a talented, creative executive? Of course they are. But in a different way and in a vastly different time frame than that of a worker.

Please note the incentive rewards of our producers weren't tied to profits. A worker's capacity to affect the bottom line is too remote. Rather, the rewards were directly related to increased productivity. And the rewards were fairly immediate - once a month, or at least once a quarter.

The achievements of the CEO and his top assistants, on the other hand, may not show up in profits for a year or a decade. Therefore the top echelon should be rewarded no more often than once a year. We provided competitive salaries and year-end bonuses which depended on improvement in bottom-line performance over the previous year. Better yet, in certain cases, we tied the bonus to the increase in return on investment over a five-year average. (After all, it takes ingenuity to make more and spend less.) Every profitable year, stock was distributed among the employees in proportion to their individual wages. The stock's value rose or fell with the bottom line.

Again no rewards were left to someone's judgement. As a result we had negligible executive turnover. By the way, in years where the results were either negative or even - no bonus or stock was forthcoming.

As for the CEO, my time frame extended to the day I would retire. I drew less than the maximum salary the IRS would allow, and, during hard times, only enough for my family. Rather than personal income, the compelling challenge was growth and stability. The fun and frustration was in getting there, not arriving. Upon developing the track record, my reward - cashing in - was fairly easy.

The day I sold my company and put it behind me, I felt good. Now a confession. Certainly the monetary reward was comforting. But that afternoon, when all the employees gathered in the cafeteria to meet the new owners and celebrate the sale, several got up and spoke kindly of my achievement, my success. Those words of recognition were sweeter than anything money could buy.

What's Talent Worth?

Beyond a person's talent, what do people who make outrageous fortunes contribute to the common good? It is hard to justify the enormous rewards many receive for their managerial skills, their entrepreneurial daring or their artistry. We are deluded to think there's no one else out there that can match their talents. A substitute's style may be different, but the results can be equally as effective.

Assuming the rewards of the most economically successful people in our society were modest, yet more than most would receive, would those people still produce? It is natural to create for monetary reward, yes, but that's rarely the deeper motivation. We excel for the love of what we do. Entrepreneurs are in it first for the challenge. Artists and scientists are self-motivated to find their truths. Let there be an upper limit to income. Narrow the spread between the richest and poorest. Compel the high earner to invest the excess in ventures that benefit the common good. We might well become a nation of philanthropists.

The Successful Team

When I read Peter Drucker's article in the *The Wall Street Journal* that Ford's design team has "serious problems," that GM's Saturn Division is steadily abandoning the team concept and that Procter & Gamble is returning to individual performance in developing and marketing new products, I'm chagrined. The team idea works for the Japanese and it worked for our small company. Indeed it was the major factor contributing to the successful turnaround and continuing sustenance of our bottom line.

Mr. Drucker describes three distinct kinds of teams: the baseball team in which each member is solitary and performs only in his or her assigned position; the football team wherein the players, also assigned to specific positions, act in concert; and the tennis doubles team in which neither member has a fixed position and each covers for the other. Of course, the goal of all three types of teams is to win. In a business organization the team is supposed to accomplish a specific task more efficiently than each individual within the team could working singly. Depending on the task, our company utilized both the football and tennis doubles kinds of teams. Both kinds were equally effective in the jobs performed. Both kinds elicited enthusiasm among their members and resulted in extraordinary individual, as well as team, performance. From this experience it would seem the team concept is wrongly condemned. The team itself is not intrinsically the problem that leads to disenchantment. Rather, a variety of essential, but missing, elements that promote team performance are behind it.

In all cases, the goals of each team, whether for an hour, a day, a month, a quarter, or a year, were clearly understood by each member. An hour task could involve turning out a small order for a customer. A month-long task could have as its goal the reduction of copier paper use. A quarterly task could be the development of an incentive system or the design of a new and better production line. And a yearly goal could be specific bottom line or return on investment (ROI) improvement.

Before we had teams, only individuals were assigned to such tasks and, accordingly, held responsible. This approach failed to take into account that each person was dependent on others within the organization to achieve results. (In fact, some employees might choose to compete rather than cooperate with others.) Only one person had the most incentive, and often the only incentive, to perform an assigned task.

In a team, every individual on whom the accomplishment of the task relies, has the same purpose - the reduction of copier paper use, let us say. But to assemble a team, define its goal and allow it to proceed is hardly enough - especially in our individual-oriented, competitive culture. Without motivational and disciplinary elements, ineffectiveness and discouragement are eventually bound to develop.

Three conditions had to prevail: the team members individually and jointly had total control over their assigned tasks; their results were objective and measurable relative to a mutually agreed upon constant; and the teams were substantially and frequently rewarded - monthly where possible. Under these conditions both kinds of teams worked well.

Of course all this was achieved in a congenial plant-wide atmosphere in which the employees were privy to the company's financial statements and often participated in major company policy. The employees had learned through such openness to trust management.

Eventually every employee of the company, save the president, was a member of a team - either a football or tennis doubles type. The company as a whole became a team of teams. It took no great leap for the separate teams to discern they owed their rewards, their good fortune, to the entire company working in unison.

Our conclusion: individual performance is perhaps most valuable and even necessary where original expression is needed - as in the invention of products and the development of theories. But in the world of process, group creativity, given full sway and meaning, is far more effective.

Curing a Dysfunctional Company

A recent PBS radio broadcast reported kids from Asian boat families transplanted to the U.S. out-perform American-born kids, even in our poorest schools. The broadcast further explained each child felt he or she had to do his or her best for the sake of the family. Hearing this, I immediately understood the startling change for the better in the performance of my employees during the recession of 1981-82.

For the first 15 years during which I was CEO, our company was dysfunctional. Employee turnover was high, productivity low and management was under continual stress. During the last five of those 15 years I experimented with a range of management ideas - the four-day week, employee ownership, quarterly profit sharing, flexi-time, elimination of time cards, frequent all-employee meetings, you name it - trying to break the pattern of our mediocrity. Upon implementation only a few of these measures produced significantly favorable results.

Implicit in these attempts was my desire to give every employee cause to identify with the company, to feel, as the boat children feel, that all of us were really one "family." The employees seemed to acquire a sense of this when we began routinely revealing and openly discussing our P & L at quarterly meetings. Everyone learned the truth, the bad news as well as the good, which tended to make us inclusive. It helped clarify the problems at hand and define our goals and made everyone more receptive to the necessary corrective steps.

But while this may have unified us and encouraged trust, we still clung to the crass competitive ways we were taught as children to practice and admire. It is the American style. Just as it is American to do something just good enough, forsaking perfection. We learned how costly that could be in the space program.

The Asian kids, the broadcast went on to say, devoted twice the time to their homework as did the American-born kids. Having been denied educational opportunities reserved only for the elite in their land of origin, these families placed the highest value on education. Surprisingly, the larger the boat people's family, the higher the kids' grade scores. After the evening meal, while the parents cleaned up, the kids sat around the kitchen table and studied together. There the older kids helped the younger ones with their homework. Suddenly my mind's light flashed again. Well, how did my company get the employees to cooperate with each other? And how did we motivate them to strive for perfection and efficiency?

Given the employees' acceptance into the inner sanctum, and given their participation in making many policy decisions, it started with the installation of team incentives. First in production, then in all departments where performance could be measured. At the time, I had attributed our phenomenal turnaround, despite a recession, to the effectiveness of the incentives. But wasn't this too simplistic? Was the monetary reward the sole reason behind our great bottom line - eventually 15 percent on sales? What incentive did the boat people's older kids have to help their younger siblings?

While certainly we didn't want to crush the individualistic spirit of our employees, we hoped that after exposure to team effort they would conclude on their own cooperation was more beneficial to the individual after all. It turned out they voluntarily went out of their way to help each other, to the point of learning the other person's job. In other words, the team concept, reward aside, encouraged a generosity of spirit. So far as individual excellence was concerned, the team allowed for it, displaying appreciation for outstanding performance through respect. We never found a rare and exceptional worker resenting the average performance of his or her average colleagues or refusing to share.

Until I listened to that broadcast I hadn't seen the subtler implications of the dynamic prevailing in our company. Our good fortune continued for five years after the recession until we were sold. To the people who bought us, I referred to the company's culture as a way of explaining away our success. Such an attribute is hard to incorporate, especially since the buying enterprise had its own unique culture to impose on the new acquisition. Upon visiting the company a few years after the sale, I found nothing left of our innovative ways.

At first 100 souls, then 35 more or less producing just as much, we had a singleness of purpose, a sense of belonging, of sharing, the courage to be honest and open, a cooperative spirit. Money, reward, as I see it in retrospect, was only part of the story. This also suggests that for maximum performance an organization has an optimal size, one in which the individual can still feel important. Our company was like a highly motivated boat family that had once known hard times.

The Innocent CEO

At the behest of their CEO, three executives (two concerned with employee relations, the other with operations) flew 1,600 miles to my home in Maine, "To find a miracle that will solve our problems," as one put it. They wished to learn about incentives and the open company. With sales of about $200 million, their consumer durable-goods manufacturing company hadn't been profitable for the past three years. With the recovery from the current recession lagging, declining sales were anticipated for the next year and possibly beyond.

In the session's first hour, in an often emotional unburdening, they described the company's plight - the intense price competition in the marketplace, an in-house war between marketing and manufacturing, a lack of new and innovative products, an overworked CEO who, while dividing his time between divisions, appeared indecisive and out of touch, a costly out-of-control employee benefit package, middle management and worker insecurity, and a vice president of operations who thinks he knows all the answers.

Then to my surprise, during the second hour, as I listened without comment, they also offered a passel of solutions.

*By restricting the product line to more popular items, manufacturing costs would drop due to longer runs, enabling the company to meet or beat the competition. Stop trying to be "all things to all persons." Find a niche and stick to it.

*The power struggle between marketing and manufacturing must end. Neither should be dominant. Rather, recognizing their common interest in achieving a favorable bottom line, they must together develop both a marketing and manufacturing strategy.

*Invest in R&D. Design a fresh, new line. Cease being the industry's follower and recover their historic position as the innovative leader.

*Without delay appoint a full time president who will be totally involved. He must be a decisive, upbeat leader. One who, through openness, will build confidence among the employees in the company's future.

*Explain the company's dire situation to the employees (all non-union), and reduce the benefit package.

*Replace the head of operations who is near retirement age. Replace the opinionated, rigid marketing vice president.

As an objective neutral party, I was well aware I was hearing only one side of the general problem. Yet from much of what they said it wasn't hard to cull fact from opinion. Furthermore, they prescribed specific actions which, even if not entirely correct, were bound to be better than the prevailing no-action policy.

When I presented an outline for an incentive plan, they tossed it aside. Since the workers were already compensated on the basis of individual incentive - piece work - the plan I suggested would serve no purpose. The workers were bound to resist an hourly pay system, a necessary adjunct to any worker incentive plan. Anyway, labor was barely 10 percent of total cost, a poor place in which to mine for savings.

What about adopting the open company concept, tearing down the barriers to communication and boosting morale. All three agreed the owners, a Blue Chip American corporation, would never consent to divulging detailed financials to the employees. This would require overhauling their entire costing apparatus. A standard cost system was used to measure the efficiency of the various elements within the organizational fiefdoms. No bottom-line figures were available; no one knew how much a particular manufacturing facility actually made or lost.

Then why, I asked, did they come to consult with me? They seemed to know what was wrong and how to set it right. Their reply: Because their president asked them to. In truth, they expected to find no answers different from their own.

Throughout the day, during which they reiterated their complaints and remedies, they consistently excused their CEO who, they pointed out, worked 80 hours a week doing his utmost to tackle the problems. He had appointed people from various departments to form task forces for the purpose of recommending courses of action. However he didn't know, at least not yet, they weren't cooperating with each other. He had also assigned an executive search agency to find a president 18 months before.

From my own days as a CEO, I had learned to stay in daily touch with all my key people (and be visible to as many employees as possible) if for no other purpose than to show an interest in their existence. I got them together often to make sure they were in harmony and adjudicated any differences between department heads immediately. I couldn't possibly do the job competently as a part-time leader. I had learned the company mirrored my personality and style, that I gave it direction and stability. I was the eminence behind every triumph or failure or injustice. Yet these executives seemed unwilling to admit their CEO was the prime source of their company's problem.

The Japanese have the right idea: when an employee commits a crime against the company, or pulls a major blunder, the top man has to bear the brunt, possibly resign. That the CEO is the true culprit is implicit in this act. This is as it should be.

When the session was over, I said: "Your CEO sent the wrong people, you know. He should have come." They smiled, then we all went out to dinner and had a good time over lobster.

CHAPTER VII

THE SALE

Rotating CEO's

Selling was becoming more and more difficult. The geographic markets we were serving had become saturated. Most customers preferred vendors that were located in their own backyards - no more than 250 miles away. Therefore our plants in the midwest and northeast were too far from the less competitive markets on the west coast, the southeast and eastern Canada. Our grand plan was to have three more satellite plants located in those crucial locations. It seemed the only way we could grow. But such logic was more easily perceived than realized.

Financing was no problem. Money was loose. In fact our bank had been encouraging us to borrow more and be more daring. Staffing was no longer a problem. We had sufficient managerial talent in-house to spare. And it would give some of our best people the opportunity to realize their dreams of more autonomy. But the expansion never happened. Why? Because the CEO did nothing. I did nothing.

The business was fifteen years old. Times were good and the future seemed bright. I was in my mid-fifties, in good health. I envisioned many years at the helm, guiding my company through unknown challenges. But something held me back. In truth, I had run the gamut of my ideas and ability. All my creativity had been expended over the prior fifteen years. In a sense I was like the scientist who makes one great discovery in his lifetime and that's it. Although I suspected I had reached my limitations, it was an issue I refused to face.

Many CEOs think of themselves as kings and have no wish to abdicate after ten or fifteen or twenty years or when they've grown old. They either can't or refuse to see they're doing their companies a disservice. By ten years at most, they have nothing new to offer. They've given their best and what remains is their worst. Sometimes abdication is the gracious way out.

For the CEO to acknowledge this, to say that his job is done, can be a terrible admission. Or so it would seem, except that his job needn't be done at all. It's only done at his company. The time has come for him to move on to another place or perhaps to something new where his experience and knowledge are fresh. Just as his replacement can revitalize his company, he is now free to do the same elsewhere or in another capacity. In so doing, a CEO may become only chronologically old but remain emotionally and mentally young and alert. As a result he adds years to his ability to contribute wisely to whatever cause he takes on.

Only in retrospect do I see how my limitations hindered my company. In my late fifties, I found reasons other than those limitations to sell the business. When the sale of the business was consummated I thought my days as an entrepreneur were done. But I was wrong. After a few years, my entrepreneurial spirit was challenged anew. An opportunity presented itself. I'd self-publish. My readers would be my customers. Again I'm coping with the bottom line and it feels good.

The Crossroad

When a mature business is going well, the CEO faces a crossroad. Either he thinks he's infallible and becomes a victim of the "Success Syndrome," which ultimately leads to his demise, or he recognizes the smoothness won't last. If he subscribes to the latter, he may also conclude it might be the best time to get out.

As our success gathered momentum and the company grew steadily, it seemed with little effort, I figured I could take it easy at last. Having struggled for 15 years building the business, I had grown weary. I discovered success brings no respite. The CEO never has it made.

Many CEOs, no doubt, cash in for what they believe will be more security. Not this one. I did it with trepidation. I felt I had more security while I was in business, beating relentless inflation and controlling my destiny - at least to some extent. Money in the bank was at risk to inflation; money in the stock market was at risk to incompetent managers. Money in my own company remained secure and never stopped working.

Approaching 60, I had to decide whether to grow or not to grow. After trying the latter course briefly, I was bored. I sensed that if the company stood still for long it would eventually wither. Furthermore, our best young people, in the midst of their most energetic and creative years, refused to tolerate the status quo. Either I provided challenge and expanded, or they subtly threatened to quit. As for myself, I suspected, having expended my entire quiver of ideas, I had finally reached the limits of my leadership ability.

From my days as an employee elsewhere, I observed most CEO's tended to stay beyond their time, especially those who were principals. They had lost their drive and applied only tired solutions to their company's problems. I saw my time had come to sell the company. It was time, not to retire, not to play golf or sail or travel, but to go on to something new - to write about the lessons of the past, to serve a purpose larger than the accumulation of personal wealth.

Many CEO's would perish were they to take off their boots. Their work is their purpose for living. To them I suggest forfeiting all monetary gain. While still at the helm they can devote themselves to cultivating new talent in every sphere of their business just for the pleasure of it. At last they can return to basics. After all, money had never been the primary issue; it had always been people.

The Role of a CEO's Life Cycle

I write from the point of view of a man in his mid-60s. I write about another, my father, when he was the same age. Only now do I understand how he must have felt about me, his 30-year-old son, when we were in business together.

Years later when I was a salesman with another company I'd frequently witness a bitter argument between the company's president and his son. Usually the father expressed in colorful terms his displeasure with the son's decisions. The son, embarrassed by my presence, would meekly defend his position. He stood no chance of course. His father had the clout. He had been using it from the day his son was born.

While I tended to sympathize with the son, I realized from experience the arguments were loaded with complex feelings and had nothing to do with the subject at hand.

My father owned and operated a small custom upholstering business of five or six employees in a medium sized northeastern city. From the time I was 10 - when I proudly swept the shop floor - until I was 18 and had learned most of an upholsterer's special skills, I worked in the business. In our employer/employee relationship, my father and I had our ups and downs. By the time I graduated high school I had decided against a future in the business. After service in World War II, and then graduating college, I still had no desire to join my father. Instead, I wished to emulate him and to make it on my own. He was my entrepreneurial model.

During the next few years, while employed at companies in the midwest, I rose to positions of increasing responsibility as a manufacturing manager. Thus I proved my capability to myself. However, the desire to be on my own constantly nagged me. My father's heart attack elicited the opportunity. He asked me to come "home" and take over his business. He had to ask only once. It was a business I knew. You might say it was in my blood. I returned to the northeast full of enthusiasm and exciting ideas on how to make the business, whose sales had remained stagnant for years, grow.

My father had promised (in writing) he would step aside and I would have full managerial authority. However, though it was unsaid, he retained control of the purse. During the Great Depression money had come hard to him. Fearing debt, he refused to borrow to invest in his business. Yet, since times had changed, I failed to understand his caution. Too young to be conditioned by the Depression, I had the typical postwar mentality: borrow because it's cheap and pay back the debt with inflated dollars.

I spruced up the showroom, added an interior decorating service, (under my talented brother's supervision) and began an advertising campaign in the local newspaper. In less than three months my father refused to support the cost of advertising. Two months later he was back to running the business as always, as if I weren't there. Feeling useless, and following many bitter arguments over the need to invest and grow, I quit. (My brother quit some months later.)

In his 60s, near the end of his career, my father merely wanted to coast until he could no longer work. How could he let go? His business was his life. Barely 30, I was just beginning my career and wanted to build a business that would become my life. We were at opposite ends of the career cycle, and so, of course, were our points of view. He feared risk; I thrived on it. At the time, I thought he was narrow, selfish and rigid. He thought I was an irresponsible daredevil.

Move forward 30 years. I was CEO of a plastics materials business many times larger than my father's upholstering shop. My best and brightest employees in key positions were young - in their 30s. To keep them happy I'd have to provide a dynamic environment or lose them. They came forward with big ideas: build more satellite plants, develop new products, maintain an aggressive advertising campaign. With plenty of cash and a bank encouraging me to borrow, money certainly wasn't a problem. Risk was. I was feeling tired after the years of tribulations and preferred the status quo. I was suddenly my father, and my people were me.

My father had hung on and now I understood why. It was comfortable. It was all he knew. His small business had allowed it. I would have liked to, but that luxury wasn't possible. My business was certain to decline were I to cease trying to grow - to continue avoiding risk. Indeed, the greater risk was not to grow. My only option then was to sell. That meant retirement. Could a man who had been active for so long be content sitting on the sidelines? It was frightening to contemplate.

In business we are aware of, but often ignore, the different needs of our employees at various ages. We often fail to put these differences to best use. Simply: employees in their 20s and 30s are producers; in their 40s, creators; in their 50s, coasters; and in their 60s, grazers. My father and I misunderstood each other in large part because we were unsympathetic to each other's stage of life. In business our expectations of each other depend on such an appreciation. It's a distance that took me more than 30 years to close.

Coping With a Rebound

In 1982, after two years of slowing orders and stagnation, our company began to experience a gradual uptick. Our customers were increasing the size and frequency of their orders. Though we remained wary - after all, this might only be a temporary blip - we saw a glimmer of relief. As I walked through the plant on my morning tour, I was smiling again and telling everyone, that while caution was in order, a recovery could well be in progress.

Sure enough, we soon saw it was. We could tell the rebound had staying power when our customers showed less concern about prices than our capability to deliver on time. After a few months, when the rumble of employee dissatisfaction with the excessive overtime drifted up to my office, we could hardly doubt we were experiencing the consequences of a full-fledged recovery.

Our industry was classically cyclical, often swinging between over-supply and shortages. But no recession had hit us as hard before. In earlier recessions the effects had been muted. During those days the industry was still young, still at the cutting edge, and perhaps growth was unstoppable. But the most recent recession had struck our industry well into its maturity. Furthermore, there were vastly more players competing with each other.

At one point the 1981 recession had come dangerously close to doing us in. Our panic and sense of helplessness at that time were seared in my memory. It must never happen again. Somehow we must make ourselves less vulnerable. One way would have been to stop growing and let the profits accumulate. But we were too entrepreneurial to pursue such a safe course. Moreover, to stagnate is to die - if not from competitive pressures then from boredom.

Another way to increase our safety would have been to diversify our product line. Fortunately, our aspect of the industry encompassed a broad customer mix: from plastic film to carpet fibers, from wire insulation to toys. Unless a recession is long and deep, not all industries suffer to the same extent at the same time.

The field was segmented into commodity and specialized product lines. We could broaden our line or launch a research project to develop new products. We did both.

We invented a patentable product in solid form that, for some applications, was better than our standard one. Matching the competition, we also developed a product in liquid form that had begun making inroads in the industry. This involved some new machinery. But we avoided expanding the range of our regular manufacturing capabilities and sought customers in new industries for whom we could make products with the equipment we had. As time passed, this policy proved too conservative. By not upgrading our equipment, we missed servicing entire industries with highly profitable products that our competitors, with newer facilities, were taking on afresh.

Those were the early Reagan years when the capital gains tax was still low, the inflation rocket was sputtering and talk of a reduction in the income tax held promise of sustained prosperity. It seemed certain the rebound would become a solid upward curve. Our company, for the first time in its 15-year history, became not only debt free, but a net lender. It owned CDs paying 12 to 15 percent, just about what it was then earning on each sales dollar.

Though we didn't realize it right away, we had a problem: success. Everything we did went right. It seemed uncanny. In a couple of years we got used to it. Then it was downright dangerous. Why do we humans so often fail to realize that prevailing conditions can't go on forever? Change is the single most constant feature of life.

In good times costs tend to ratchet upward, often those we thought we had under control. The hourly workers (we were non-union) pressed for increases above the cost of living increase they routinely received each year. Even the salesmen, whose pay was in part based on commission, and who were selling and earning more than ever, demanded an increased base salary. Though material costs also climbed, we could easily pass them on. Still, the most we could do as new competitors entered the scene was to hold our prices and, in some cases, drop them. Our best choice was to "make it up in volume," as they do in supermarkets. That meant grow, grow, grow.

Ours was a special case: I had no wish to take on the task of becoming a larger organization. So I sold the company at what I thought was the high or near high. Recently, when I visited the main plant, business was down drastically. The cycle had turned. The capital gains tax was historically high, the income tax had climbed and money was tight. It was 1981 all over again. Change. Depend on it.

The Education of a Businessman

"What's your secret?" asked the executive V.P. as he compared our low operating costs with his. His large corporation was about to buy our company. The two were similar in terms of products, equipment, even some of the customers.

Did we have a special process? He hadn't detected it as he toured our plant. Did we pay our people less? He found we actually paid them more than he paid his. Was it the economy of size? Shouldn't being bigger result in smaller unit costs?

It's our culture. Don't disturb it, I warned. If you do, the company will become like any other and you'll have wasted your money.

Not until then had I understood so clearly what had contributed to our organization's enormous success. It wasn't due to any technical superiority or special skills. It was the atmosphere, the ethos, the openness, the sense of security, the mutual respect of employees and management, the desire and willingness to experiment in striving to do things better. It was, in short, our attitude.

For 10 years before it was sold the company was a virtual management laboratory. We were in a constant state of change, going from one enthusiastic high to another. Not everything worked. For a few it was so exhausting they had to leave.

To most it was a turn-on, and our turn-over was negligible. When, on rare occasions, I reported to work at 7 A.M., I was surprised to find some employees had already voluntarily preceded me more than two hours before their normal starting time. In some instances, we had to order people to use vacation time.

Today I read sad tales of how the Japanese, the Germans and the nations of the Far East put us to shame by applying their indigenous ways to producing our unused inventions. Even the American companies that struggle to catch up don't quite make it. The target is elusive. After all, the American way is not the Japanese way, or the German way, or the Korean way. Nor should it be. We are ourselves.

Yet our small company seemed to have mastered the lessons learned by the successful foreign companies despite our peculiarly American individuality and impatience. We were self-taught and made tons of mistakes in the process, each one instructive.

Based on things we did wrong, some of the salient lessons I learned were:

*Don't trust everybody; don't mistrust everybody.

*Don't agonize over firing someone who isn't performing.

*Don't make a decision that can be comfortably delayed. Give it time to gestate.

*Don't try to solve every problem; given time some go away by themselves.

*Understand an employee can never appreciate the risk the owner/CEO takes, or know his or her solitude.

*When you're on top, never think you have it made.

Based on things we did right, the lessons I learned were:

*Constantly question the status quo in every aspect of the business.

*Though we can't control the world outside, we have a good measure of control over the one within our walls. Always look within first to take action.

*The traditional autocratic American company discourages independent thinking and responsibility; the democratic company encourages free expression and innovation.

*The employees have the answers to problems, or will find them, if asked. Outsiders, consultants, can never know a company as well as its employees.

*From the CEO to the janitor, everyone can be a decision-maker, and most employees wish to be.

*Problems having to do with material things - machinery, processes, products, etc. - are easy to solve but people problems aren't.

*Business is not so much making and selling products as managing human relationships: employer/employee, supplier/customer, customer/vendor, company/community, taxpayer/IRS.

*Because things have always been done a certain way is good enough reason to consider change.

*Greed begets distrust. Generosity is repaid in trust again and again.

*Offer substantial and immediate reward for measured excellence, and the bottom line will grow beyond imagining.

*Make every employee a member of an incentive team, and cooperation will replace competition, slackers will stand out and be forced to quit, supervision will cease to be necessary and innovation will become marvelously rampant.

And I tore down the wall of my illusions.

I acknowledged that:

*My modus operandi was to minimize risk.

*I valued security above all else, and it dangerously bred inertia.

*Entropy reigns, life isn't smooth: when things are going well, watch out. It isn't normal.

*Most of the time, at a deep level, I was running scared, afraid of a slowing economy, of key people leaving, of a competitor's new product, of technical advances in our field, of the very nature of business which is little more than an elaborate crapshoot.

Perhaps the most difficult thing I learned was nothing endures. Our company had to change or it would die. It had to grow, not necessarily in the American way of becoming bigger, but by getting better, more efficient, innovative and exciting. Otherwise it would stagnate and our best people would leave for challenge elsewhere.

This meant some of us had to go (either out or down or sideways) because after we had given our best there was nothing left. Some stopped giving by 50, others were still giving at 70. But energetic souls, those still in their 20s, 30s, and 40s, were beating against the door of those whose contributions were no longer significant.

After almost 20 years of service, I knew I numbered among the latter. It was my turn to leave. And I knew the employees realized I had lost the drive to roll dice. My last mission was to ensure that the company would continue to thrive without me in the same thrilling manner to which all of us had become accustomed.

Two years after selling the company, I visited the principal plant. The atmosphere had changed. There was a new calmness. No one complained, but no one raved about conditions either. I asked the production manager how things were going. Fine, he said. The plant was spic and span, everything ran smoothly. Then, sadly, he added that no one told him anything beyond what he had to know to do his job. He was bored, turned off, because most of the major decisions he used to make were now made by others from a central office.

Everyone's wage was increased and the incentive plan was scrapped.

The executive vice-president had missed my point; he had heard but hadn't listened.

How to Sell a Business and Survive

Only after I decided to sell our business, did I discover why. Aside from personal reasons having to do with my desire to do something new, I soon realized the timing was perfect. It was 1984, midway into the go-go Reagan era and before Congress had increased the capital gains tax. (They were debating it at the time.) Having recovered nicely from the recession at the beginning of the decade, the company was showing unprecedented earnings of 12 to 15 percent on sales in an industry that rarely does better than 5 percent.

Intuitively, I had chosen to sell at the high. Prospective buyers didn't mind because they were buying into the future. Always insisting on five-year sales and profit projections, they were most willing to accept my extrapolations based on the most recent two years' performance. Clearly, the upbeat economic climate had conditioned them to see gold at the end of our particular rainbow.

I also learned to make the sale happen was far more complicated than I had imagined. Though everything seemed right - the economy, the company's profile and the buyer's willingness - the details killed deal after deal. Negotiations involved the following features:

*Finding a mutually agreeable price.

Price was strictly a matter of opinion and rarely reached the negotiation stage until the very end. Some buyers saw the asking price - an opinion based on a multiple of earnings typical of our industry - as outrageous, and others saw it as a bargain. Either it was within range of the buyer's mindset, or discussion was irrelevant. Either the buyer wanted the company, tasted it, or he remained only a curiosity seeker.

In other words, the right price for the buyer, though a crucial consideration, wasn't by itself enough to bring about a sale. Nor was it for the seller, because I hadn't known until the eleventh hour how much less I'd be willing to take. (I had originally envisioned a figure of about seven or eight times the average earnings of our last five years.) It was like having to experience the advances of a number of wooers before I could know which one I'd "give" myself to.

*Would the buyer give cash or notes or both? What would I take?

Some buyers were earnestly interested individuals who had strong management records with large corporations. They were always enthusiastic. Initially, negotiations went smoothly. We shook hands on the deal. First they had to raise cash through private investors or banks. I waited. They failed to come through. After a few such episodes, I opened all future discussions with the blunt question: "Item number one, do you have the money?"

More important than price was the structure of the deal: again details. I wanted cash. Some buyers offered only their stock, or a small amount of cash plus long-term interest-bearing notes. Others made the payout contingent on the company's future bottom-line performance. Having witnessed the loss of fortunes by entrepreneurs who had sold their companies for stock, or on a contingency basis to corporations that later went bankrupt, I knew better than to go for such deals. (The long-term decline in the dollar's purchasing power is quite enough. Who needs stock?) Shouldn't my risk years, those years of building the business, be over? Furthermore, I had no penchant for starting again in my late 50s.

*Does the buyer want the CEO to stay, act as a consultant, or make a clean break?

I had no wish to stay. Having done things my way for 20 years, I knew I could never do them somebody else's way. This factor quickly eliminated parties who weren't familiar with our business - and most of them weren't. Most buyers were surprisingly lean on management talent and they had little to offer other than capital - of which we already had plenty.

*Will it be a stock deal or an asset deal?

Most buyers wanted an asset sale which would give them a tax advantage and the seller a disadvantage. In an asset sale, the buyer would not have to worry about writing off goodwill, but the seller would have to pay taxes on the recapture of all leasing costs and depreciation going back to year one. In our case, such taxes would have been enormous. In a stock sale the buyer would be compelled to write off goodwill over a too lengthy 30-year period (according to the law then), but the seller would suffer no tax consequences beyond capital gains. Obviously, I insisted on a stock sale.

*Who will assume what liability?

The buyer wished to withhold a certain sum for a year as my guarantee all was what I said it was. Having hidden nothing, I agreed. The buyer also insisted I personally be held responsible indefinitely for all IRS claims made against the company for prior years.

*Is the timing crucial for the buyer? For the seller?

It was November 1984. I wished to sell before Congress passed the 1986 tax law that would have increased the federal tax on capital gains, then 20 percent, to a substantially higher income tax rate. The possibility of the new law retroactively taking effect haunted me. The buyer was most accommodating and pushed the deal through for a December signing.

The deal we finally made had it all. The buyer, being in a related business, understood ours: they didn't have to "learn the ropes." Management was ample; in fact the would-be president participated when the discussion reached a mature stage. The buyer also preferred a clean cash deal. But the price, the price: the buyer began with a ridiculous offer and was told so, and then returned a few days later with a still low, but reasonable one. It was two-and-one-half times our net worth and about five and one half times earnings. That was in line with the industry's multiple at that time.

The structure of the deal was so superb from my point of view, and our company was such an ideal fit from the buyer's point of view, neither of us could walk away. It seemed both parties were under a compulsion to hammer out a compromise. They would pay more, I would take less. On behalf of the employees they would expand the company and not exploit it. I would serve as consultant for a year and not compete for five years. We shook hands and everyone was pleased.

So far so good, right? Wrong. The calamitous details, like a stubborn virus, lived on. Earlier I had informed the buyer that part of our 5,000 gallon oil tank may well be partly buried beneath our neighbor's property.

Suddenly it became a sticking point. The buyer's executive vice president warned we had better correct the situation or the deal would be off. (The actual dialogue was far more pungent.) That such a minor detail could abort the agreement came as a shock. With my dander up, I refused on principle: the deal was off. After all, they knew about the oil tank before we shook hands.

A few days later the buyer's board chairman called. Could we settle the matter over lunch? Indeed we could: it was settled over tuna fish sandwiches in three minutes. The oil tank would be a non-issue. I insisted the chairman be present at the final signing in the event similar details arose that would require on-site attention. I discovered a truth: always deal with the top decision maker.

At the signing I discovered another vital truth: know your interest and be your own master. The buyer stipulated I be held responsible for any tax liability that might develop from prior years. My lawyer refused. Their lawyer remained adamant. We were deadlocked. But, having been audited twice by the IRS during the previous five years, I knew we were clean and had no cause for concern. My lawyer was about to kill the deal. Taking him aside, I acquainted him with the facts. He cautioned me against the risk I would take were I to consent to the buyer's condition. If there's one thing I've learned in business, it's that nothing worthwhile comes without risk. No doubt, if I had asked my lawyer to protect me against dying, he'd have tried. Lawyers, I concluded, aren't businessmen. We closed the deal, and now seven years later, I'm still intact.

Ask me whether I'd sell today, I'd say: No way. The time isn't right and the capital gains tax is too high. But if I were 20 years younger I'd be out there looking for a bargain.

Evening the Score of Caveat Emptor

After reading Bryan Jamison's essay in *The Wall Street Journal*, "Hunting the Elusive Creature, the Big Deal," on the vicissitudes of trying to buy a small business, I, as a one-time seller, feel compelled to offer a view from the other side.

For three years our employee-owned, plastics processing company of 60 souls (cash rich and getting richer) was courted by scores of business brokers and "interested parties" large and small, rich and poor, responsible and wild, sincere and just curious. Eventually we grew weary of the strain of baring our audited figures, customer lists and manufacturing facilities. Most lookers were seeking the impossible: a guaranteed future of ever-increasing sales and profits to the end of time. Then, as we were about to give up, serendipity intervened: The right outfit came along from out of nowhere.

Certainly Mr. Jamison is justified in complaining about sellers who present figures consisting of "one- or two-year-old handwritten tax returns". But we found even an informed and thorough presentation ineffective.

Our 20-year-old company prepared a bound sheaf explaining virtually anything a buyer would want to know about us - including an unadulterated history, graphs of the industry's fortunes over the same period, quarter by quarter financial statements, 10 years of audited figures, a business biography of each staff member and five years of "realistic" sales and profit projections. Even so, after flying thousands of miles, often in corporate jets, most prospective buyers who sat in my office to make a deal were more often than not disbelieving, suspicious, or at best, skeptical. A few secretly questioned my employees to find out whether I told the truth.

Virtually every prospective buyer asked the same three questions:

*Why are you selling if the company is doing so well?

During the most recent five years sales grew at a 10 percent rate with profits at 12 to 15 percent on sales. I was approaching 60 (but looking and feeling younger) and ready to retire with no family to take over the business. In the event of my death my wife was ill-suited to run the company. Nor would she do as well selling it as I hoped I would. To those who seemed unconvinced, I bluntly added the right time to sell is at the highest point. This always worked.

*Wouldn't the company fall apart without you at the helm?

For the prior three years, a capable, well-organized staff made all the day-to-day decisions without my guidance. I confined myself to major policy and keeping track of morale. But no one bought my story. How could I prove that in preparing for a future sale I had succeeded in making myself almost superfluous?

*The third question, really a series of related questions, would arrive late in the exploratory process. How firm is the asking price? (Answer: fairly firm.) Will you take paper? (Answer: no.) Will you stay aboard and accept a salary as part of the deal? (Answer: no.)

Buyers tend to dance around the core questions. Bring them up at the beginning and buyers will change the subject. When they're finally asked and must be addressed, the dreamers and bargain hunters reveal themselves.

Mr. Jamison discusses the exorbitant asking price according to "the more than meets the eye approach." But the right price is not the same for every buyer. A perceived need adds to value. Our asking price was based on the prevailing industry multiple, as best as we could determine, of the average of our past five years' after-tax earnings. Fair, rational, like the stock market? Yet it really bothered me many offers were made based on book value alone, as if the intangibles such as the struggle to build an organization, our years of trial and error, our technical expertise, our reputation and industry contacts, our unique culture, all that had made us successful - didn't count.

Oh, there were some who yearned to own "a gem, a find, an ideal fit" like us. They wooed us over a dozen visits, and besieged us daily on the phone, yet couldn't bring themselves to commit. Their extreme caution was stultifying.

When an owner tells Mr. Jamison, "the business really makes a lot more money than what is shown on the statements, but he or she wants to keep taxes down so not everything gets reported," he may well be telling the truth. Many small-business owners whisper to friends that they've cheated the IRS out of fortunes. Common ploys are to expense what should be capitalized or have maintenance employees do repairs on your home at company expense.

What constitutes the true profit figure? That is typically the most controversial question. Being closely held, we were in the habit of keeping our bottom line to a minimum to avoid - for one thing - doubly taxed dividends. Therefore, we distributed a share of our pre-tax profits (beyond that which we retained for reinvestment and operating capital) as salaries and production incentive bonuses, and as contributions to the employee stock ownership plan (ESOP). But we failed to convince most prospects such sums would, under their circumstances, drop to the bottom line rather than appear as costs. Yet they had to admit a division vice president could be hired to run the company for less than half my salary.

A direct conflict between buyer and seller would invariably arise on the nature of the sale: the buyer would insist on an asset rather than a stock purchase. From our point of view an asset purchase was absurd, but some buyers were adamant.

Mr. Jamison's negative experience with brokers is exactly opposite ours. Those we encountered were sophisticated, supportive and realistic. They usually brought forth candidates who were a feasible fit and who professed a willingness to consider our terms. Only one broker, whom we refused, wanted a ridiculous up-front fee without even a guarantee of performance. And one persisted in smoking cigars in my office despite a posted "Thank-you for not smoking" sign.

Frequently when meeting a principal buyer through a broker, strange things would happen. The buyer would express unanticipated reservations or his requirements would suddenly change. He could not have read our presentation. Or had he confused us somehow with another company? We would be planets apart, much to the broker's embarrassment.

One deal almost materialized: an allegedly wealthy corporate executive plunked down a substantial non-returnable binder before "sewing up" the bank. While he missed the first deadline, then an extended second one, we lost two other interested parties waiting in the wings.

How ironic the valid buyer who finally appeared turned out to be a neighbor. No broker was involved. The deal actually was born three years earlier when, by chance, I happened to meet the chairman of a semi-competitive company at a local lunch counter. If ever I decided to sell, I should look him up, he said. At the time it was out of the question. I forgot our discussion.

He hadn't. When the word of our interest in selling reached him, he sent his emissary. After three months of relaxed and free-wheeling negotiation, I discovered what our real priorities were. We found ourselves more flexible about price than we anticipated. Indeed, the structure of the deal, the fact it would be for cash - a stock, not an asset, purchase - the factory building would go with the business at a fair price, and the buyer intended to retain all employees and invest in the acquisition rather than exploit it as a cash cow, turned out to be as important as price. After both parties compromised on the final figure, the deal was done in less than a month.

Good luck, Mr. Jamison, in your search. And expect to be surprised.

Taxes and the Businessman

Our accountant, a wise and reflective man, used to say, "Never make business decisions based on tax considerations." I found his words appalling. In fact, in making decisions in which there could be tax consequences, I instinctively took them into account.

Of course, what our accountant meant was taxes should be extraneous to the successful running of a business. He also used to say: "Don't complain about taxes. Be happy you're doing well enough to have to pay them." I couldn't argue with either precept, yet I thought he had it wrong. Most accountants, I suspected, would make poor entrepreneurs. Though we businessmen do our utmost to minimize risk, we are just as committed to maximizing our take, and taxes work against that effort.

I discovered taxes were not an uncontrollable item after two years in business. It was time to leave our rented space in a run-down district of a small city. We looked to expand to an industrial park where we could build a facility to suit our special needs and have room for future growth. Though the city's industrial park was located far from a major highway (proximity to which we considered important since most of our incoming raw materials and outgoing shipments were made in bulk and transported by truck), we would have moved there had the city given us an inducement to stay. After all, most of our employees lived in and around that community. Instead, its civil servant, the property appraiser, offered to "take it easy on us" - if we would "make it worth his while."

Meanwhile, a small town 10 miles away presented us with a location in an industrial park on an interstate highway. But the clincher was a property tax break - no taxes - for the initial five years there, just when we would need relief to build our business to meet the added cost of expansion.

The consequences to us and to that community proved salutary beyond anyone's expectations. During the next seven years, from an initial 10,000-square-foot plant we grew fourfold and from 10 employees we became 100. Our ultimate financial contribution to the town was substantial. And because of the town's prior consideration, we always paid our property taxes with a smile.

As we struggled and prospered, we made other more or less tax-based decisions. We installed anti-pollution equipment before it was mandatory, encouraged by a state law exempting it from sales tax. And to avoid double taxation we never declared a dividend that would have rewarded our employee-owners. Rather we plowed the money back into tax-free and tax-deferred benefit plans.

Indeed our very decision to install an ESOP, in which a portion of our profits (returned to us through an employee trust) would be deductible, was largely driven by its tax advantage.

But perhaps my most momentous decision after starting the business was selling the business. That was partially, though significantly, dictated by tax concerns. At that time my personal income, as well as the company's, was taxed at 50 percent. I was drawing the maximum salary the IRS would tolerate for a company of our size. Any additional personal income would have had to derive from doubly taxed dividends. Thus I had no financial incentive to make the company grow, especially for a man approaching 60. I would have simply had to work too hard for what was left after the government took its share.

On the flip side, the federal tax on capital gains was then effectively only 20 percent. By 1984, when Congress was formulating a new tax law, I pushed hard to sell before an anticipated increase in rates took effect. I succeeded, though I moderated some of my demands on the buyer to do so. I beat the 1986 tax law and saved a small fortune.

So I often ignored our wise and reflective accountant's advice. In fact he used to say that though I sought his counsel, I usually did precisely the opposite to what he recommended. Obviously he was a keen observer, as well. But what would I have done differently under present tax law? Income rates are low relative to what they had been - though still not low enough to maximize incentive. And capital gains rates are nearly confiscatory for a tax of that nature.

I would have delayed selling and let the company coast for another two or three years to see whether Congress would correct its mistake as disinvestment occurred around the country. After confirming the unlikelihood of this happening, I'd sell anyway. My personal need to unload had priority over tax considerations. But I would have driven a harder bargain with a prospective buyer to compensate for the higher tax.

Suppose there had been no towns around to offer us a tax break during that first expansion. Would we have moved to the industrial park on the superhighway? Certainly. Not only was the location superior, so was the town's political climate. Taxes were secondary.

Now in my post-sale maturity, I can say our accountant had been right all along. Not that tax considerations didn't matter, but they came second. It had been a hidden assumption all along. When we get down to it, the business of business, and the business of life itself, prevails. And that's as it should be.

The Business Six Years After the Sale

Three years have gone by since my last contact with the company's employees. It seems fitting to update the reader on the company's present status.

How has the company fared these past six years? Has it lost its identity during the merger with a much larger entity? How many of the old employees remain and are they happy? What has happened to the culture? Has the open style of management survived? What about the incentive plan and our unique sales compensation plan?

When I called the office (the old phone number still remained in effect - a good sign) to announce the date and time of my visit, familiar voices enthusiastically greeted me. As I drove up to the plant, I observed the sign on the facade had a new company name, but under it appeared our old one, a token to the past. Obviously, our old identity had been eclipsed. When I entered the office I was welcomed with warm hugs by a skeleton office staff that existed only to service that facility which was devoted strictly to manufacturing. Administrative and sales functions were performed at corporate headquarters in another location.

But the staff, having been given considerable autonomy in what it did, was happy. The production manager shook my hand warmly. A good sign because I recalled his unhappiness during my last visit three years earlier. At that time management had taken away his autonomy and, in fact, had imposed their indigenous methods and techniques into his operation against his advice. It was an ego thing, he figured. The new bosses seemed to feel they knew more than the people they bought. In the meantime, however, seeing their system was inferior to the one our company had developed over the years, the parent gave up, allowing the production manager to pursue the old proven methods. That is to their credit. Now he too was happy. "No one bothers me anymore," he said. "I do what works."

As I toured the plant, I was surprised to find so many of the original workers still there. To a person they smiled, greeted me by name and shook my hand. Many thanked me for "selling to the right people." Though the new owner abandoned most of our innovative management methods (but retained our liberal benefits or bettered them), the employees felt they were dealt with fairly. Perhaps most gratifying was their recognition of the company's loyalty and concern for their welfare. Despite the fact business was slow, no one would be laid off: work was found to keep everyone occupied.

While on the tour, I heard my name paged over the PA system. Shades of the old days. Answering the phone, I was greeted by the hands-on, proficient manager of the midwest plant who had heard I was visiting. His facility, I learned, was more profitable than ever, now doing as much business as the larger one in the east used to do. In a few months he would be expanding into a bigger building in a neighboring town.

Our two plants had now grown to five from coast to coast through the company's further acquisitions, with a sixth under construction in the south. My former second-in-command was now the manager of one of those plants. Of course, the parent had appointed a president to replace me from within its own ranks.

It was apparent little remained of our culture - just as a more powerful Western culture overwhelmed the culture of our native Indians. The corporation's closed style had obliterated our former openness. Reflecting the chairman's personal approach, the parent was more hierarchical than we were; it drew more lines, separating people from each other. There was no sense of the organization as a cohesive, solid entity, but instead one made up of independent discrete parts. No longer did the employees have contact with the very top. Some had felt like children neglected by their parents.

But I felt satisfied the new owners had fulfilled the wishes I had had for our employees and had taken the company further than I could or would have. It seems I did right. My only complaint: the place could be tidier, it needs a paint job. Now if I were still CEO I'd --- . Well, what's the point, eh?

CHAPTER VIII

SOME VIEWS FROM A DISTANCE

Borrower Versus Lender,
Businessman Versus Retiree

Any ambitious entrepreneur knows raising capital is toughest when starting out. In fact, a bank may not even be willing to talk to him or her, as in my case. Having been someone else's employee until then, I had no "track record." But thanks to the Small Business Administration (SBA) which guaranteed my virtually worthless signature, and my silent partner's more valuable one, a bank finally listened. (Painful though it has sometimes been, I've been more than willing to pay federal taxes ever since.) For the next 15 years I became a habitual borrower.

Borrowing for business made just as much sense as having the largest possible mortgage on one's home. With the value of real estate, capital goods, inventories and personal income ever increasing, inflation was my other silent partner. (Based on history the current hiatus in inflation is only temporary.) Today's enormous loan became the next day's easy-to-handle debt. In fact, to not borrow was to miss out and possibly fall behind. It was the post-World War II thing to do. (At the same time, my father, a small businessman and a product of the Great Depression, feared for my debt-laden life.)

As our small business grew, so did the opportunity to expand our product line. That meant purchasing expensive equipment and adding more manufacturing space. Taking success for granted, with hardly a thought to the risk involved, we presented our plan to the bank. Our loan was quickly approved.

It was a time when most banks were sound and there was no credit crunch. In fact, the bank's major concern was making sure we had sufficient collateral. It was not in the least concerned that we should pay back the principal. In subsequent years, borrowing became easy, almost fun. It was like having a rich uncle always at the ready. We screamed in outrage when the interest rate hit 6 percent. But that hardly deterred us. We knew, as did the bank, our return on capital (ROI) was better than 25 percent.

Those were the days of low interest rates and high inflation. The borrower's life was a good life. Then everything changed: I became a lender.

After 17 years the company stopped expanding, a substantial cash surplus accumulated, and all debt was repaid. We ignored the bank's entreaty to borrow again and resume growing. Meanwhile, our accountant warned: either use the money for further expansion, declare dividends or pay more taxes. Instead, we sold the company.

Quickly I discovered a lender's life bears no resemblance to a borrower's. As the latter I was accustomed to using money for specific purposes over which I had control. I was always confident the investment was secure and would produce a decent return.

As a lender, having more money than I needed, an obviously enviable position most would say, I felt lost. There was no specific, creative use to which I could put it. Instead I found myself with a host of unanticipated worries.

Suddenly inflation, once my silent partner, had become my most feared enemy. Preserving capital was the number one goal. The investments (Treasuries) that preserved capital offered little protection against inflation. The investments (stocks) that stood to beat inflation did so at the risk of losing capital. This was something entirely outside my entrepreneurial experience. No longer could I have it, as I had in business, both ways: relatively risk free and capital enhancing at the same time.

Compelled, to some extent, to dealing with stocks, I found myself unprepared for the irrationality of the market. When I discovered consensus was rare among the soothsayers predicting its course, I became confused. I lost confidence entirely when I observed the opposite to what the majority predicted often happened.

Worse, I found myself lacking the up-to-the-minute essential knowledge about a company one needs in order to judge its future. The management, wishing to present a positive picture, often withheld salient information that would eventually be revealed only after I had purchased the stock. Most companies, both large and small, in which I invested, frequently gave me unhappy surprises. But as CEO of my own company, I played with loaded dice and surprises were few. The stock market seemed more like a mindless crapshoot by comparison.

The experience of dealing with stockbrokers has been perhaps most disturbing to my entrepreneurial psyche. When I was a businessman, in most transactions both parties usually won. If the customer failed, a part of our business also failed. Not so with the stockbroker who stands to win when I win and win when I lose. The transaction itself is the thing, not the thing transacted. I have a difficult time not thinking that no matter how noble the stockbroker might be, there has to be some trace of greed lurking within his soul. The system demands it if he is to succeed.

This brings me to the most troubling issue of all: dealing with the brokerage house. It seemed the house existed as a silent eminence behind the stockbroker, preferring to distance itself from the customer. Such an attitude was baffling to my entrepreneurial rationality which valued a close relationship between the organization and the customer. It was second only to getting his orders. When things went badly at the house - the monthly statement was incomplete or rife with errors, or the stockbroker had committed fraud - the house not only ignored you, it declared you the enemy.

As CEO, I saw to it our company attended to complaints immediately as a matter of policy. We also saw them as an opportunity to further cement our relationship with the customer. Our quick response showed that, even when things go wrong, we're behind him. Good Lord, how can brokerage organizations be so customer blind? I had similar experiences with three.

As a borrower I used to think the lender had it made. Now as a lender, I know that's not the case. When Polonius advised Laertes, "Neither a borrower nor a lender be," he was right on. But in our society, unless you're a pauper, you've got to be one or the other. Which is easier, borrower or lender? I only know I don't want to be a pauper.

Something's Wrong with American Business

American management is stupid. Thus spoke W. Edwards Deming, the father of participative management, during a 1991 interview on PBS. (In your 90s you can afford to be blunt and honest.)

In their 1990 book, *The Machine That Changed the World*, a five-year MIT study of the automotive industry, researchers James P. Womack, Daniel T. Jones and Daniel Roos, conclude the homegrown American technique of mass production is no longer competitive with those of the Japanese who devised and practice "lean" production. The reason: the former makes things "good enough" at high cost while the latter strives to make things "perfect" at least cost.

After a recent series of articles by this author that appeared in *The Wall Street Journal* about incentive systems and open management, I was deluged with calls and letters from CEOs across the country seeking more information. Some complained that due to low productivity, their companies' profits were dismal. In almost every case, they were seeking ideas on how to motivate their employees.

Something's wrong.

For the past 75 years we made better products cheaper and faster than anyone else. Now Japan and Germany and even some nations on the Pacific rim have surpassed us. That leaves us to excel only within specialized limits - the manufacturing of passenger aircraft, for instance, or designing software.

From the back-office performance of one's stock-broker to the purchase of a refrigerator, to having a key cut at the local hardware store, there's a good chance errors will abound and things won't work properly. When the service was provided or the product manufactured, the premise was it was "good enough." The person responsible for the bottom line, the CEO, cares. He knows better than anyone he can't do it alone. But his people frustrate him and render him helpless.

Perhaps we can assign a share of the blame to our educational system, but I suggest we look further.

Try our competitive free enterprise system. It's gone too far. Whereas we function under the principle of self-interest, we incorrectly judge what constitutes self-interest. Indeed, in making that error, we actually end up doing things contrary to our individual and our company's interest.

Why?

No one doubts we are an intensely competitive, litigious society. Indeed, our culture teaches us from infancy to compete. It does not, as the Japanese culture does, teach us to cooperate.

We stress individual performance over team performance. Even where our teams are concerned, football, baseball and basketball, the financial rewards and the kudos go to the individual stars - not the whole team - as if the star did it all himself or herself.

In business we operate under the subtle assumption that everyone with whom we must deal is our adversary. Take our employees. Don't they try to wrangle as much pay as possible out of us? Our customers: aren't they always trying to beat us down on price? Our suppliers: isn't it standard operating procedure to play one off against another to get the best deal?

And the government: who doesn't see the IRS as the supreme enemy by definition? That leaves the bank: why does it want to know so much and charge those confiscatory interest rates? Whose side is it really on? Why must a businessman's life be a constant battle?

Because we make it one.

It's a nonsensical battle. What sense does it make to compete against those on whom we depend: our employees, our customers, our suppliers, the government and the bank? What makes sense is to compete against those with whom we're directly competing: our competitors.

*The employees: let them participate in controlling their destiny and richly reward them for excellence so they'll be motivated to produce more.

*The customers: level with them, take them into our confidence, and try to give them the best deal so they can thrive and buy more.

*The suppliers: encourage them to give us the best deal by showing them loyalty and how to provide better and cheaper products and/or services.

*The government: pay taxes willingly and be grateful; no other system in the world is more conducive to succeeding in business than ours.

*The bank: realize it is our gambling partner whose fortunes rise and fall with ours.

Perhaps all this sounds too idealistic, impractical. Hardly. That's the way many Japanese businesses operate. A group of interdependent companies, including a bank or its equivalent, form a consortium called a keiretsu dedicated to the success of all.

In fact, the companies interlock, each owning a piece of the other (and sharing in each others' profits). They openly join in a total effort to develop better products, better methods and lower prices for their mutual benefit.

It is a cooperative sub-system operating within the context of a competitive system. By joining forces with those upon whom a company depends, a company is stronger and more capable of competing than it would be by itself.

What's wrong with American business is our blind "hooray for me, screw you" syndrome. This demonic attitude is invading the dependability of our products, our capacity to innovate, our effectiveness to produce, and the very quality of our lives.

For more than 150 years our competitive spirit worked well while we led a world of lagging nations. It no longer works in a world in which our leadership is challenged by determined reborn nations and creative coalitions.

Now, suddenly, we're often seen as the old boys wedded to obsolete ideas. It's time for a change.

Long live "lean" production, for mass production is dead. How many in the U.S. know this? Long live motivating the employee by giving him a voice and some degree of control. How many of us are willing?

Long live sharing a company's profit and loss statement, balance sheet, profits and ownership with its people. How many dare take this chance?

Long live a company's human relationships because this is the essence of business. How many of us realize this elementary fact?

Yes, there is something wrong with American business. How many of us accept this? Who is willing to help change it?

Where the Greenest Grass Grows

What? A Japanese businessman calling for Japanese management to emulate us? Doesn't Yoshimichi Yamashita, whose December 16, 1991 appeal for change in *The Wall Street Journal*, "Japanese Executives Face Life Out of the Nest," realize American management sees its salvation in substantially imitating the Japanese? More and more as we come to terms with ourselves, American companies acknowledge our way of doing things falls short in a global marketplace.

Our home-bred automotive companies still can't match the Japanese in quality and economy of production, even as they introduce Japanese methods. Our American hubris and readiness to settle for less than the best dies hard. The Japanese still out-gun our micro-chip producers. In sub-atomic research, our government is forced to lead and provide the capital a la MITI (Japanese Ministry of International Trade and Industry). Our jet engine companies find it necessary to join forces with their foreign competitors. As American management examines the successful Japanese model, it sees its rational approach must give way to a more "relational" one, as Mr. Yamashita would put it.

Indeed, our small plastics materials company found that the relational problems, not the rational ones, were the source of most of our troubles. We were small enough that in our managerial experiments the relationship of cause and effect was swift and direct. Though we didn't know it at the time, we independently adopted workable solutions that resembled the Japanese approach.

The assumption underlying nearly every successful outcome, largely ignored by our rational American system, was that every transaction, whether with an employee, a vendor, a bank, or a customer, involved a relationship. And to make it work it must be mutually beneficial. If Mr. Yamashita's Japan, which has capitalized so well on that assumption, goes strictly rational as we do in America, I predict its certain decline.

Mr. Yamashita makes several recommendations to his management brethren that suggest he is unaware of the pitfalls in our system.

For example, when he calls for the Japanese to Westernize their management, he must also understand he is risking bringing on the worst consequences of our adversarial culture. That includes a litigious society, one ripe for the formation of militant unions and a typically dictatorial management style motivated by short-term results. We are so bottom-line oriented that management advances hype over substance and ignores the long-term health of the company and the happiness of the individual.

I'm dismayed when I read Mr. Yamashita seeks to discourage the "Japanese concept of 'group ego'" and "company ego." For years our management strove to achieve just that by convincing our naturally skeptical, Western culture-conditioned employees that the company was open and honest and really cared for their welfare. In return we expected their loyalty and dedication to perform in the company's best interest. It was a tough sell, but once accomplished, our company began to flourish as never before.

"Recognize individual talent --- and rally around the creative spirits. Stop hammering your mavericks," Mr. Yamashita advises. It may well be the Japanese system suppresses the outstanding individual. But I would remind him the organizational form by its very nature discourages genius and independent action. Such individuals must seek to make it on their own as entrepreneurs or find a less constraining environment in which they are free to follow their own paths without disrupting others. It is the responsibility of the greater culture to provide the dynamic environment and/or the special institutions in which these rare individuals can flourish. The organization is not the place.

More than once our company had to dismiss exceptional workers and brilliant executives for the greater good and harmony of the organization. After we introduced the team concept in which reward was based on group rather than individual effort our productivity skyrocketed. Of course, those employees who were superior were rewarded accordingly, but it remained that they had to fit in or chaos would ensue.

As for the kieretsu form, which displeases Mr. Yamashita, in which a consortium of companies have a stake in each other, its monopolistic nature admittedly discourages the inclusion of competitive suppliers from the outside. It's a decided, but not insurmountable, defect. But Mr. Yamashita should know in our so-called intensely competitive Western system, most companies, in a less formal way, tend to stick to the same suppliers and are slow to adopt new ideas and products by upstarts. Our "open," adversarial system does not have the kieretsu advantage of mutual cooperation in driving down costs and improving quality between buyer and supplier.

When I beseeched our bank to provide relief after Federal Reserve Chairman Paul Volcker in his war against inflation drove up interest rates to 21 percent, I learned it couldn't care less. Indeed, seeing our profit consigned solely to servicing debt, we lost all incentive to grow and came close to giving up. Were we and the bank members of the same kieretsu, the bank would not only have been sympathetic, but would have been inclined to give us a break because it would have been in its interest as well.

Of course, I sympathize with Mr. Yamashita's criticism of the Japanese style in which individual effort goes unrecognized, where living the corporate life leaves little room for anything else, where ethnocentrism prevails and the national mind is closed to appreciating the best in other cultures. Where then does the grass grow greenest? Like him, I too would welcome a blend of "--- Japan's relational style with the West's rigorous rationalism." But both Japan and the West must not go at it wholesale; they must choose the best of each management culture carefully and adapt it to its own. How awful it would be were we to clone the worst in each other.

The Dark Side of Capitalism

The Free Enterprise system endures. We are now the economic model of the failed socialist nations. Their failure vindicates our stubborn insistence capitalism is the best way. But is it? How well does it satisfy our human needs which, after all, is what every economic system strives to do. And if our system leaves something to be desired, what can we do about it?

An entrepreneur's responsibility is to the bottom line, otherwise the enterprise fails. However, the entrepreneur's responsibility to employees, customers, vendors and the community is arbitrary and then only to the extent that these parties serve the interest of the enterprise.

The entrepreneur is free to accumulate all the wealth his or her luck and ability can generate. No one criticizes a successful business person for not sharing with the less fortunate. Rather, his or her success is admired, emulated and envied. Because wealth is power, it commands everyone's respect. Character and integrity are secondary considerations.

Our system is based on Adam Smith's principle that the pursuit of self-interest benefits the common good. History would indicate self-interest more often benefits the uncommon good. Government then intervenes to even things out. Corollary to Adam Smith's principle is the underlying assumption that what's good for business is good for the nation. In this assumption lies the nexus of our trouble. Only when a business's abuses are blatant are its actions restricted, and then only in response to the organized expression of outrage.

We are so caught up in the system we fail to realize our business ways have inflicted more subtle damage upon us. Though our businesses have scarred the landscape, polluted the air and water, and compromised our health (in effect degraded the quality of our lives), we are slow to acknowledge the system may be at fault. Who can possibly claim the interest of business - its bottom line - has consistently benefited the common good?

Business, due to its competitive warlike nature, its inherent rationality, has fostered individuals alienated from family, from self. We are a people obsessed with a warrior mentality in which human feelings and values are consumed in the battle of the bottom line. In the name of making a living we forsake our dreams, do what the boss says, and become a member of the crowd. Such features of business do not benefit the common good.

Our culture is rife with hype, fakery and outright dishonesty on an enormous scale. Through media advertising business propounds half-truths. It makes unsubstantiated, deceptive claims. Advertisers seek to manipulate our minds rather than try to convince us by means of honest argument and reliable data. This in pursuit of a better bottom line. We are demeaned by it. We are so confused that we value appearance above substance. Are we a nation of fools to be so responsive to falsehood? Can one say this condition wrought by business has accrued to the common good?

Business commits us to poor health and early death. The large restaurant chains purvey nutritionally harmful menus. Cigarette companies thrive while we die of cancer and heart disease caused by their products. Our food-producing corporations hawk cereals stripped of their God-given nutrients and lace them with sugar. Soft drink companies provide nutritionally empty formulas that destroy our teeth. For the sake of the bottom line, business compromises the very health of our nation. The cost to us, the so-called beneficiaries of Adam Smith's self-interest, is enormous.

Let's reverse our assumption. Make it instead: what's good for the country is good for business.

Conditions in America and the rest of the world are far different from those prevailing in Adam Smith's day. Our world is smaller and incredibly crowded. Due to our numbers and our advanced technology, the pollution is of a volume and a nature never imagined. No longer is there room enough in the nation or the world in which to hide the waste. We live in its midst. There's no escape.

Beyond the vast numbers of people, of industrial plants, of homes and office structures, of retail outlets and malls, is the sheer size of things. The scale of our cities, of our farms, of our institutions, our government, is so great we feel lost, dehumanized. Each of us has become but a mere grain of sand. No wonder we are alienated from each other. Yet we impact on each other as never before. As we protect and enhance our special interests we compromise the common good.

If the good of the country were to come first, business would not be allowed to forsake it for the bottom line. A business would reclaim the land it spoiled, reforest the hillside it clear-cut, utilize available technology to eliminate air and water pollution. It would apply its resources to replace harmful products with beneficial ones.

In this scenario some businesses would go under. New ones would rise. Prices might climb for they would include the cost of maintaining the high quality of our lives. But not necessarily. Were our government to abandon the taxation of capital, it could insist business apply those funds to the benefit of the common good. If a business's interest and that of the entire nation ceases to be coincident, the business either gets its act together or fails.

To counteract the deceptive practices of business, the government has intervened by insisting on honesty concerning products. Given time, the most forceful regulator is the market itself. The public eventually learns the truth. The American automotive industry never stood a chance once the word spread that Japanese cars were superior. Price was never an issue. Our cars were cheaper.

The lies and omissions business spreads about its products merely validates the public's cynicism. The pity is business is slow to learn its lesson. It still seeks to foist inferior products on us at higher prices by seeking protection against superior foreign competition. The solution is simple: become as good or better. If you can't, then fail. A business producing mediocre goods with mediocre employees does not benefit the common good. The quality of our lives suffers. Mediocrity is pervasive in our society - from our schools to our products and services.

Must the drive for profit necessarily cost us self-fulfillment? It has been demonstrated time after time an enlightened management policy that encourages employee participation, drawing on the creative powers of all within an organization, enhances the bottom line. A human business approach which recognizes the whole person results in increased productivity. A dictatorial, secretive management style so prevalent in America works, but less efficiently. In terms of human happiness it fails absolutely.

Theoretically, our elected government is designed to meld local interests into that of the general interest. More often, however, it does the opposite and sacrifices the unrepresented common good for the interests of business - the farmers, for instance. At times it also sacrifices business interests and the common good simultaneously, as in the case of banks and the S & L debacle. Our federal representatives solicit the largess of business to retain power. Consequently they subscribe to the precept: what's good for business is good for them is good for the country.

Thus government-owned water is sold to large farming corporations below cost at taxpayer expense. Does it make sense to grow thirsty rice crops in the desert valleys of California? Pollution laws are ignored in the case of large employers. Timber, oil, gas and minerals on public lands are made available at low cost to businesses. Much of our wilderness has been desecrated. To protect special industries, energy policy is either non-existent or not in the common interest. The government is only the sometimes friend of the people. More recently it has had ambivalent feelings towards business. Seemingly without a clear policy, it helps some and harms others. It needs a consistent philosophy based on what's beneficial to the common good.

Most businesses eventually die, but many, especially the giants, transcend time so long as their products and services remain current. Such businesses look beyond the present into the infinity of generations. To prosper long term they must concern themselves with the health and welfare of their employees, their customers, their vendors, and their sources of capital. They are all necessary participants in their success, all beneficiaries of the common good. Any business that does otherwise will be, in the span of history, short-lived.

The narrow view that what's good for business irrespective of whether it's beneficial to the nation, is obsolete. The abuses are now too obvious. Business must awake to the logic of the common good, see to it that its interest and that of all the nation's people - yes, of the world's people - coincide.

In Conclusion

From our company's beginning with one employee and myself in a small garage with a dirt floor and a leaky roof, to its sale in the comfortable seven figure range, I have learned much about business. I also learned what not to do and about many things that are right to do.

I have learned four important lessons. One is that a business depends on human relationships. Everything that benefits those relationships with which the business is concerned benefits the business. Failure to nurture those relationships, whether with employees, customers, vendors, banks, investors, the community, or the nation, damages the business. This fact may not be obvious, as it wasn't to us at first; it's like seeing that one is poor in a world of only poor people.

Another lesson is that the bottom line is the truth, and it must be heeded with least cost to human happiness. A business's ultimate goal is to transcend a good bottom line and promote the welfare of those to whom the business is responsible. Once managers stop with the bottom line they compromise their humanity and the happiness of themselves and all involved.

The third lesson is that nothing in business lasts, including the business itself. Sooner or later it dies or loses its identity. A business is extreme and constantly in flux, more so than life. Indeed, business is life in fast motion.

And the last lesson: eventually the demands of a growing business surpass the capability of a CEO to meet them wisely. When this happens the bottom line is a good indicator. At that time the CEO must step aside or leave if the business is not to suffer.

After selling my business, it never occurred to me I had anything to say, that what I had learned from the experience would be valuable to others. I had taken our company's experimentation and achievements for granted. Only after *The Wall Street Journal* had published my letter to the editor as a piece in their Manager's Journal column did I realize how unique (yet universally applicable) my experience had been.

Letters and phone calls from businessmen and women across the country responded favorably to that first article and to many subsequent ones over the past few years. This has encouraged me to impart to others whatever insight I have acquired in taking our conventionally managed American company, a dysfunctional company prone to crises, into the realm of an enlightened, satisfying, smoothly functioning enterprise. I hope American business will adopt the simple principles my business followed. I also hope businesses will expand them and go beyond what we did to make a business organization a happy, more secure and productive place in which to work and be creative.

EPILOGUE

The CEO in Retirement

It's as if I had won the lottery. Now I possess mostly cash or cash equivalents and my net worth is unequivocal. Until now I had never known what I was really worth because my company's value had been undetermined. Being well off and having investments which bring in substantial sums each year without having to lift a finger gives me a feeling of freedom that I have never known before. I no longer need fear that a competitor will threaten my income or that the tribulations of the economy will seriously erode it. Best of all, I needn't suffer to earn it.

After I sold the business my personal accountant asked what I was going to do with the money. He wasn't asking how I was going to invest it, but rather how I was going to live the rest of my life.

"You're a survivor," he said, "but now that you don't have to fight to survive any more, I ask you, how are you going to survive?"

That's a valued advisor for you. He knew just what to ask. Zingo!

I've stripped myself of all responsibilities, even the overseeing of my investments which I've assigned to a professional advisor. Money and business are no longer a concern in my daily life. Instead I tend the garden and sail and travel with my (former) wife. But I still rush around: to the post office, to the gate at the air terminal, to meet friends for an evening out. Somehow I act is if I'm driven and still not free.

My wife complained that I was driving her crazy. "You miss the business, the daily excitement and challenge and being a boss. You don't know what to do with yourself."

"Not at all," I said. "If the chairman called me today and said, 'Here, take back the company for half what we paid for it,' I'd tell him, no dice."

"Then, what's going on? For God's sake let up on yourself, let up on me. You run around like you're meeting a deadline every hour. What's wrong?"

"Nothing's wrong. Absolutely nothing."

But I knew something was. An author - I don't recall who - once said, "I don't know what I really think until I write it down." To discover what was wrong I wrote my thoughts in the form of the following essay.

IS THERE LIFE AFTER RETIREMENT?

Everyone around the long table had just finished signing reams of legal documents transferring ownership of my small employee-owned company to a corporate behemoth. I was elated and overflowed with feelings of affection and goodwill.

"Have a happy, good life together," said the smiling board chairman. He was a vital man in his mid-seventies who rose from his chair to embrace my wife and then me. How odd to hear such words. They seemed more applicable to a young man just starting out, than to me. After all, I had just turned sixty.

With a sense of wonder I looked into the faded, peaceful eyes of this wrinkled man who was so much older than I. "And you, when are you going to retire?"

"The race is too much fun," he said. "I'm going right to the finish line."

Having spent over two years trying to sell my company, I had had time to prepare myself psychologically for life after work. When I decided to unload my company, I had no intention of banking the fires of enthusiasm within myself. Rather, I stopped asking "What am I doing?" and began asking "Why am I doing it?"

My job seemed to be done. True, I could have made my enterprise bigger. But the quantities of life - homes, cars, money, status - were sufficient and it was time to concentrate on the quality of life that I had sacrificed in the quantitative wars.

Since I'm no longer a businessman, people want to know what I do now. When I fill out questionnaires, beside OCCUPATION I have trouble putting down "retired." When meeting new people, they usually ask, "What did you do before?" I find it hard to answer. What bothers me is the world wants to know what I am rather than who I am.

My wife, whose contact with the world has been more circumscribed than mine, is now ready to burst out and see what's out there. But I resist. During the traveling we've already done - trips to the Virgin Islands, Southern California, Paris, and Washington, D.C. - I can't wait to return home. But once I'm here, home isn't yet home; the roots haven't taken hold.

From my study window, between the tall hedges behind the house, I can glimpse tantalizing portions of the perennial garden I've been busy restoring after ten summers of neglect. For those ten summers I had vowed that one day when I left the rat race, I'd make the garden beautiful again, a haven for the soul. One crystalline morning this spring, kneeling in the soil in the shadow of the hedge while planting a bed of peonies, I became overwhelmed with sadness from the beauty and peace around me and my eyes filled up. What was this?

It happened again one brisk, shimmering June afternoon while I was gliding across the bay on a broad reach in my small catboat. I was exhilarated with a wonderful sense of abandon, a feeling I used to dream about having and that I can now have practically at will. Yet, after ten minutes I couldn't endure it any longer and felt suddenly afraid and empty and headed back to the mooring. I've hardly sailed since.

I have to admit my retirement isn't working. I'm unaccustomed to the freedom and security I now have. Life is too easy. This isn't my reality. For years I seemed to thrive on fear of failure. I survived the deadly competition and the outrageous swings of the economy. My success was proof that I was worth something. No one can take that away. Surely it's an integral part of me forever. But what else is there? Is selling the business my swan song after all?

I've looked to once-successful men like myself, now retired, for the answer.

"How did you adjust to all the freedom, the glut of time?" I asked.

"I've never been busier," one former CEO of a company many times larger than mine answered. "In fact, I often wonder how I ever managed to find time to work before. You'll adjust soon enough."

But none of them said they were fulfilled by what they were doing.

One thing I've discovered is what I call the law of compensating activity. With time cheaper and more available I find more things to do in order to use it up. Recently I stopped wearing my watch. The old day-to-day deadlines are gone. But I have more time to ponder that big deadline looming ahead in the misty future.

The other day the nursery delivered twenty-five boxwood shrubs for a border, part of my ten-year garden improvement plan. I immediately took the wheelbarrow and the spade and went out in the sun. I worked like a zealot planting them one after another.

"What are you trying to do?" my wife said, "The whole ten years in one?"

"Certainly not," I replied. "They were there to be planted, so I did."

Then I realized what was driving me. I needed to show results. I need the satisfaction of pure visible achievement for my labor. Part way through the project, something unusual happened. After removing my soggy hat and salt-streaked sunglasses, I noticed a robin dipping its beak gingerly into the birdbath. Two brilliant poppies caught my eye. I watched the breeze sweep across the hedge of tall ancient arborvitae like a wave. Then, erasing time, I lay on the grass leaning on an elbow. I did nothing but enjoy the sweet ambience of that time and place. In those moments I had, however briefly, forgotten what our culture and my upbringing had taught me, and what my internal drive had forbidden me to ever do. Never in the past would I have squandered precious time doing "nothing." Every moment was dedicated to meeting the limitless demands of my company. Was this new experience and the joy it elicited what I had missed and needed all the years I had been in business?

APPENDIX

Computing a Hypothetical Incentive System

PRODUCTION:

Historical Standard: 100 widgets/hour
After Incentive: 125 widgets/hour
Number in Team: 5

Operating Cost/Hour: $50.00
Standard Cost/widget = $.50
After Incentive Cost/widget = $.40
        Difference = $.10

Total Production/month: 20,000 widgets (125x8x20 days)
Additional Profit/month: 20,000 x.10 = $2000
Division of Additional Profit: 1/3 to team, 2/3 to company

Distribution to Team: $2000/3 = $666/month
Distribution to Each Member: $666/5 = $133/month
If a Member is absent 3 days: 17/20 x $133 = $113.05
   Other 4 employees: $138
After Incentive cost/widget: 666/20,000 + 40 = $.43
Savings: $.07/widget or 14%

SERVICE:

Standard Job: 4 hours
Incentive Job: 3 3/4 hours
       Gain: 1/4 hour

Operating Cost per Hour: $30.00
            Job Gain: $7.50

Daily gain for 10 workers @ 1/4 each = 2.5 hours = $75.00
Additional Profit/month: $75.00 x 20 = $1500
Distribution to Team: $1500/2 = $750
Distribution to Each Member: 750/10 = $75/month
Savings: $3.75/hour or 12.5%